T0146592

HAPPINESS
NO MATTER WHAT!

*The Essential Seven Principles
Program for a Happy You*

Monica Belizan

BALBOA.
PRESS
A DIVISION OF HAY HOUSE

Balboa Press books may be ordered through booksellers or by contacting:

Balboa Press
A Division of Hay House
1663 Liberty Drive
Bloomington, IN 47403
www.balboapress.com
1 (877) 407-4847

Because of the dynamic nature of the Internet, any web addresses or links contained in this book may have changed since publication and may no longer be valid. The views expressed in this work are solely those of the author and do not necessarily reflect the views of the publisher, and the publisher hereby disclaims any responsibility for them.

The author of this book does not dispense medical advice or prescribe the use of any technique as a form of treatment for physical, emotional, or medical problems without the advice of a physician, either directly or indirectly. The intent of the author is only to offer information of a general nature to help you in your quest for emotional and spiritual well-being. In the event you use any of the information in this book for yourself, which is your constitutional right, the author and the publisher assume no responsibility for your actions.

Any people depicted in stock imagery provided by Thinkstock are models, and such images are being used for illustrative purposes only. Certain stock imagery © Thinkstock.

Print information available on the last page.

ISBN: 978-1-5043-6717-2 (sc)
ISBN: 978-1-5043-6719-6 (hc)
ISBN: 978-1-5043-6718-9 (e)

Library of Congress Control Number: 2016916689

Balboa Press rev. date: 12/12/2016

To: Luciano, Bianca, Calista and Victor, constant reminders of the depth and colors of true happiness.

TABLE OF CONTENTS

ACKNOWLEDGMENTS

This book is the culmination of my very long and passionate search for what is real happiness and how to attain it, and how to make it a permanent attribute in our lives. It was a long road that in the end led me to understand that happiness is the call of the Universe for us to become kinder, more joyful, creative and peaceful tenants of the planet.

That quest of decades was solely mine, but I could never have done it without the immense knowledge and wisdom of my many gifted and generous teachers. They unveiled to me ancient knowledge, spiritual philosophies, millenary healing techniques, personal experiences, and up-to-date science, so that I could at one point take my own path with confidence and trust, knowing that I was walking in the footsteps of giants.

Some of my most influential teachers have long since passed away, including Paramahansa Yogananda, Meishu Sama, Buddha, Muktananda, and Krishnamurti. More recently passed is dear Wayne Dyer. I revere them and owe them immense gratitude.

I am blessed to have had and still have contemporary teachers, including Dattatreya ShivaBaba –Babaji as Wayne

Dyer used to called him— who for years advanced me into the power of the mantras and the meaning of exuberant connections with sacred archetypes, a true teacher and healer; I am eternally grateful for his being in my life. Yoshiaki Kato who taught me the healing arts of Meishu Sama. Neil Walsh who really wiped off me all sediments of religious guilt and dogma as we watched the whales in Alaska. Jean Houston who instilled in me the perfect "why not." Eckhart Tolle who drilled in me a sense of tremendous "now" urgency. The list of the wise souls whose generosity and wisdom made and still make inroads in my mind and heart is long, almost as long as is my gratitude for all they give and teach.

I am uniquely indebted and grateful to Deepak Chopra. I have been studying his teachings since the late 90's. I met him in his La Jolla center and never again was my mind the same. He gradually but surely showed me a way to live that never left me, and for that I will always love him. Later on, his teachings at the Chopra Center provided me with the backbone of my spiritual life. It became orderly, pointed, and profound. The Chopra Center and its great teachers became my second family, a place of knowledge and wisdom. It helped me help my people in a much more profound way.

I am thankful for Balboa Publishing Company; they were the ones that convinced me I could write this book. They were right. The team was very supportive and patient, and went out of their way to be helpful. And they were always cheerful!

I would not have been able to produce this book if I did not have my editor, Susanne Dunlap. Not only did she tame the heavy "Argentinean accent" of my writing, but she also became my good friend. Needless to say she was also very patient. I guess I needed a lot of patient people around me.

Lastly, I want to thank my son Luciano and my daughter Celina. They have always been completely supportive of my work and endeavors—although sometimes they were a bit uneasy about my distant travels and for them at the time "strange places and people..." They have always been, are, and will always be the love of my life and for that I am eternally grateful.

But the biggest gratitude goes to LIFE and all the riches it pours on me and all of us every day!

PART ONE

THE ESSENCE OF HAPPINESS

When I was younger I was given an assignment:
to write what I wanted to be when I grew
up. I wrote one word: HAPPY.
When my teacher told me I didn't understand the assignment,
I told her she didn't understand life.

- John Lennon

1

E verything you think, say, and do in your life is propelled by an unending quest for happiness. Yes, it is a bold statement, but if you really think about it: the pursuit of happiness guides everything you do, from the most basic decision about what to have for breakfast to the most complex and consequential decisions about your marriage, children, career, and buying a home.

This desire for happiness is what brings every single client that shows up in my life-coaching practice. Regardless of the reasons my clients give me for why they are seeking help, what they are really looking for is the peace of real happiness. Most have gone through life expecting that the right job, partner, house, degree of affluence, or recognition will bring them happiness. Many have turned to psychotherapy, feel-good techniques, positive visualizations, and/or several kinds of yoga. Others have explored the teachings of the Law of Attraction, among others. Still more have spent thousands of dollars on self-help books, retreats, and conferences.

All those are worthy efforts that point in the right direction. They can lead to a degree of happiness and moments of contentment and hope, but after a while, the feeling evaporates into wistful memories and a sense of loss. And in my experience, it cannot be any other way because they do not lead you to discover and connect to the real, authentic source of happiness. That is why when my clients come to me, they still feel a deep emptiness that they are not sure how to cope with.

This book will lead you to understand what happiness is in all its depth, and, more importantly, it will teach you how to align with it. It will give you the knowledge and the specific practices that will transform you and your life. Happiness will no longer be unattainable.

You have had, and most probably often have, glimpses of how happiness feels: the sweetness that you feel in the love for your children or partner; the peace and joy you experience when spending time with a true friend; the hypnotic enchantment you surrender to when listening to your favorite piece of music, or when you immerse your body, mind, and soul in the beauty of a sunset. Those are all wonderful experiences, but they are occasional exceptions to the rule rather than the main fabric of your daily life. They are fleeting moments that often only put the sadness or emptiness you feel in the rest of your life into stark relief.

But true happiness is not intended to be a special exception. It is part of who we are, integral to our being. All we need is to learn how to release it, how to make it not an exception but part of every day of our lives.

I have called this book *Happiness No Matter What!* for one simple reason: To show you how to unveil a deeply felt state of happiness that persists *no matter what* is happening in your life—when your heart is broken, when someone you love is diagnosed with an incurable illness, when you're alone, when you're broke.

I know this is possible because of my own personal experience of using the Seven Principles Program for myself and teaching it to my students and clients. These Principles grow out of one simple truth: that happiness is your natural core essence. It lives inside you, it *is* you. You don't have to achieve or acquire anything to get to happiness. You don't have to look for it anywhere. You only have to learn how to live in alignment with your Self.

These seven Principles are not at all obscure or esoteric. They can be understood and learned by anybody who is willing to spend some time peeling away the layers of debris and rust that have buried their connection to their inner core of happiness.

I wrote this book guided by an urge to help you uncover and untangle your connection to your essence, to show you how to allow the light of happiness to shine within you once again and be reflected in your life and in the lives of the people around you. This book is an invitation to allow yourself to become the happy person you might not have thought was possible.

The journey starts here. I invite you to engage with me in the Seven Principles Program. Each Principle will guide you to your real core and the practice that follows each Principle will instill in you habits that will lay down an immutable foundation of happiness in your life.

Crossing the Bridge: My Path to Happiness

Happiness did not present itself to me as dramatic revelations with parting of the skies and bolts of light shining down. It was a result of a long, long voyage that took many turns with hills to climb and roads to walk.

That road began when I was a little girl of about eight. Even at that age I had a frequent nagging thought, or perhaps a feeling, that there was something wonderful out there that I was not able to grasp, a certainty that somewhere there was a hidden meaning to life that I could not see. I remember looking at myself in a full size mirror and checking the back of the mirror for the answer to my unformed question. Later this thought unfolded into deeper questions about the purpose and meaning of life.

As I grew up, I studied, contemplated, and searched in whatever way I could to discover what it was that my life was supposed to mean. I became very obsessed with this search, although I called it different names, looking at it from different angles according to where I was in life at the moment. I went from writing angst-filled poetry to immersing myself in the study of psychology and the international mechanisms of politics and power, and explored many avenues in between.

Yet after many years of deep study and work, I realized that this quest for understanding through the intellect had not delivered any real answers. I decided that I had to take a different approach, and I submerged myself in the teachings of the ancient sages of Vedanta, the Buddhist and Japanese traditions of the East, and the enlightened Judeo-Christian thinkers of the West.

I not only studied them, I immersed myself in them as much as I could. I have had—and have—the blessing of learning from the best of today's spiritual and philosophical minds, and practicing with true masters in ashrams in India and temples in Egypt, Israel, Japan, and Europe. I have experienced many places rich in mystery and wisdom all over the world, and of course in the United States from New York to Arizona to Hawaii.

For about two decades I learned and practiced many modalities and had experiences that were profound, enriching, and also challenging at times. But in the end, I always felt that none of these experiences answered my questions about why I was here, what was the purpose of my existence.

My life was indeed rich in experiences, but deep at heart I knew that there was a big piece of the puzzle still missing. I felt alone and frustrated, confused and distraught. I started to feel sorry for myself. I didn't want to study anymore, and although I learned to and still do love and respect the many gods and goddesses who became my daily partners, I did not want to chant to them anymore, or energize my chakras or yoga my body and mind. I felt myself entering a long, empty tunnel with no exit door, no light at the end.

Since I didn't know what else to do, I decided to do nothing.

I had no idea where I would be going from there, or what it would mean, if it would mean anything at all. The only certainty I had was that I had to be alone, in silence. After a while the stillness of the silence started to feel better and better. I felt more at peace, more whole. I began to feel that all was well. I didn't know at the time that what I was doing was surrendering my questioning to the stillness of my mind, to that place of knowing that had been covered by my relentless pursuit of the meaning of life.

And one day it just happened!

On a late summer evening under skies of incredible beauty, I was walking quietly on the Key Bridge over the Potomac River in Washington, DC, alone with myself in the middle of the city. I was crossing the bridge with no particular thoughts in my mind when all of a sudden I was overcome by a "knowing." I had the absolute certainty that we are here on this planet, in whatever country, in whatever situation, no matter our shape, color, sex, or age,

TO EXPERIENCE HAPPINESS, TO BE
HAPPINESS, TO BECOME HAPPINESS.

After all my searching for some complex meaning of life, I suddenly understood this simple truth: We are here to be happy. Our purpose for being on this Earth is to know happiness in person and to welcome it. Our life's mission is to understand what happiness is, to make it a constant in our life, to embody it, to live it.

If someone had simply said that to me I would probably have dismissed it as a joke. We come all the way here to this planet to be happy? In any other context it would have seemed trivial, if not absurd. But in that moment it was an unequivocal knowingness that simply felt right to me and has never left me.

This "knowing" was so complete and fulfilling that I made it my mission to figure out what true happiness is, how we can experience true happiness, how we can become happiness regardless of what life brings to us. At the same time, I started to sense that my own true happiness did not stop with me but rippled out, influencing everybody around me—indeed, contributing to the well-being of the planet.

It is with deep reverence that I now share with you the results of my search and experience. I hope that you learn from it as much as I did so that you too can change your life into happiness.

Happiness Defined

Most people define happiness mainly in terms of things they want to have: financial resources, recognition, love, health, beauty, glamour, charisma, stability, friendships, belonging, spiritual connection, and so forth. Yes, those can be associated with happiness. But by themselves they are not happiness; they are temporary, pleasurable experiences that come and go.

True happiness is an emotional, physiological, spiritual, and intellectual state of being that is whole, balanced, complete, content, clear, calm, peaceful, and joyful. It is a constant at your core that you can feel and live from in the midst of whatever your life circumstance might be at the moment. And it can only be so because *happiness is a state of consciousness*. It is the natural state of a healthy mind.

This truth does not negate life. Living with a joyful state of mind doesn't mean you don't feel pain in yourself and in others. It doesn't mean that sickness and tragedy can't strike you at every turn. It doesn't mean that your heart can't be broken in a thousand pieces or that you are immune from betrayal and abuse.

What it does mean is that when you are rooted in your real core, aligned with your essence, you are able to feel the pain, hurt, sickness, death, and loneliness—what the Buddhists describe as, "an ocean of human tears larger than the four great oceans"—with a knowing that is full of compassion for yourself and for the world the way it is. When you are connected in this way, you witness and feel what is happening in the moment with a spaciousness that allows for a wider and more profound view of the experience.

Buddhist teacher Jack Kornfield illustrates this process by referring to Hermann Hesse's novel *Siddhartha*, which tells the story of a young man's spiritual quest. Kornfield notes that at the end of the story, Siddhartha sits by the river and finally learns to listen. He realizes that the many voices he hears in the river make up the music of life: good and evil, pleasures and sorrows, grief and laughter, yearnings and love. His spirit is no longer in contention with all of life. He has found that along with the struggles there is also unshakable joy. And this same joy can be yours as well.

How the Essential Seven Principles Program Works

The Seven Principles Program will lead you to see and feel who you truly are so that you become completely immersed in your true Self, in your most intimate essence that is whole, happy, and creative.

The Seven Principles Program will:

- ☺ **Lead** you to unravel your connection to your core, your source of happiness.
- ☺ **Instill** in you new consciously chosen life habits that will keep that connection clear and vibrant.
- ☺ **Take** you to a place of knowing that can never be broken by anyone or by anything that is happening in your life.
- ☺ **Teach** you to train your mind to be present, focused, and clear so you will be able to add richness to your life and reveal your greatness.

These seven Principles are not new to the world. They have their roots in all major spiritual philosophies of the world and the seers and sages of Vedanta. Nor are they the only ones. There are many other important principles, but I believe these seven are essential, sufficient, and powerful enough to get you started and well advanced on your path to happiness.

The Principles will become standards by which you will live your life and with which you will paint your life in the colors of joy and creativity. In time you will witness your own transformation into a more joyful, compassionate, creative, and peaceful person. You will be able to be happy even in times of hardship and pain, which is the essence of success.

The Seven Principles are not meant to affect only you, although it may at first seem that becoming happiness or being happiness is by definition self-centered. And yes, this program will teach you to make happiness your default state. It will teach you how to contact your true essence, how to open your awareness, and how to deal with your thoughts and what to do with them, and it will establish new conscious habits in your daily life. The focus is on you and your transformation. But you don't live in a glass capsule, in a vacuum isolated from everybody and everything else. You live among people, and you have a major effect on your family, friends and co-workers, acquaintances, people you hardly see, and many you don't even know. By extension, you can see that the way you feel and think has a holistic global impact.

There is a growing worldwide consensus among spiritual leaders, environmental scientists, and many others that we are on the brink of destroying ourselves and our planet. We have stretched our intelligence to incredible heights, but without any regard for our soul, our Self, our intrinsic nature. Realizing the dangerous state of the world today, we see that embracing our life purpose of being happy is not a selfish one.

Your own individual transformation is necessary not only for your benefit but for the wellness of those around you and the entire planet. Thus, the Essential Seven Principles Program will show you how you can also influence the course of the planet in an evolutionary way. You will be able to contribute to what the Bible and other major religions and ancient philosophies called *"heaven on earth"*: a world marked by happiness, peace, and compassion.

Here is my promise to you:

If you follow the instructions and practice the Seven Principles Program with commitment and determination, happiness will become the foundation of all the experiences in your life— even when your heart is broken, when someone you love is diagnosed with an incurable illness, when you are alone, when you are broke. You will live with *Happiness No Matter What!*

In turn I ask you to promise me:

1. You will suspend your disbelief, withhold judgment of ideas that may at first seem strange, and be open to the experience.
2. You will give yourself the chance to work the program and **commit** to seven weeks of practice, just a few minutes a day.

Why the Seven Principles Program Works

The Seven Principles Program is not filled with quick-fix techniques to get you to feel happy or better. It is a *transformative* process. And all transformations take time. As you gradually incorporate the Principles into your mind and your life, you *become* happiness, you *become* gratitude, and you *become* love.

Each Principle will introduce an attribute of happiness and will explain the theory that supports it. Then you will be instructed in the practice of that attribute with simple though profoundly transformative exercises. The exercises won't take much of your time but they do require that you do them with patience and dedication so that they become the solid foundation of how you relate to yourself, to those around you, and to your life.

Thus the theory, paired with the daily practice, will establish in you consciously chosen habits for a happy, healthy mind and life. As you begin working with the Principles, you will start to witness changes in your life and in yourself that will be leading you to a much happier place.

How to Become a Pro in the Seven Principles Program

- ☺ **Follow the order in which they are presented.** The Principles are cumulative.
- ☺ **Study and practice each Principle for seven days, starting on a Sunday.** Read the Principle a few times, and even if it doesn't resonate with you, suspend your disbelief and do the exercises in the Working the Principle section.
- ☺ **Go directly to the Working the Principle section** days 2 through 7 and continue to practice the same Principle until the following Sunday, when you will start working on the next Principle.

☺ **Don't judge yourself.** If you have to skip a day or so, don't feel bad. Just go back to the Principle you abandoned and practice it until the next Sunday. There might be a reason why you abandoned it, so a little extra practice won't hurt. If you feel as though you didn't get enough practice with a particular Principle, stay with it until the following Sunday.

☺ **Trust that something is working** even if you don't feel it. You are transforming, but for your transformation to last, it has to be gradual. And gradual isn't always obvious. The more you consciously exercise the Principles, the faster and more deeply they will impact your life.

☺ **Post reminders of the Principle and practices you are working on for the week** in places where you spend most of your time—your kitchen, your desk, cell phone, mirror, office, car, and so on—as gentle reminders of what you are imprinting in your mind. The more you see them, the more you will keep them in your awareness as you carry out your daily activities.

Some people learn better through listening than through reading. If you prefer to listen to the exercises, go to my website at www.monicabelizan.com and choose Working the Principles for some audio-guided exercises. You will also find additional information and suggestions on how to work with the Principles there.

Cheers to your transformative journey into Happiness No Matter What!

PART TWO

WORKING WITH THE PRINCIPLES

Transforming Your Life into Happiness
One Principle at a Time.

Sound drums and trumpets!
Farewell sour annoy!
For here, I hope, begins our lasting joy.

- William Shakespeare, King Henry VI, Part III

FIRST PRINCIPLE

Awareness: The Root of All Happiness
Training your mind to pay quality attention

The key to growth is the introduction of higher dimensions of consciousness into our awareness.

- Lao Tzu

There are almost as many definitions of happiness as there are people who seek it, and countless theories about how to be happy. In Part One of this book, I stated my own definition of happiness as a particular state of consciousness or state of mind. I also greatly appreciate the wisdom of Matthieu Ricard, the French monk whom the media calls "the happiest person in the world." He defines happiness as a deep sense of flourishing that arises from an "exceptionally healthy mind." This exceptionally healthy mind is an extraordinarily capable mind that is profoundly peaceful, compassionate, and happy.

This kind of healthy mind is not reserved for monks in the caves of the Himalayas, or for those supposedly born with happy genes. It is available to everyone, including you and me.

This First Principle is fundamental to your transformation and as such, it provides the basic structure for the entire Seven Principles Program. It will show you how your mind works and functions and will teach you how to train it and take care of it. As you apply it with practice and discipline, you will be able to transform your mind and the quality of your life.

If you are like most of us, you are probably used to looking to the outside world to understand your feelings. If you are happy, sad, focused, or unfocused, you tend to blame or praise something out there, something external. The problem with this way of understanding your feelings is that it makes you a passive recipient—life just "happens to you." By relating to the outside world in this way you relinquish control, become a victim of your circumstances and other people, and make a sustainable peaceful state of mind impossible.

Of course, outside events can and will influence every aspect of your being. But how you deal with these events is directly related to your state of mind. A healthy mind will have a more wholesome, more creative, kinder response to any given external situation than a foggy, obscure, congested mind.

A healthy mind does not negate the events that send you spiraling into sadness or fear. On the contrary, a healthy mind is fully present with what is happening to you, internally and externally. It is fully present with your sadness or fear, and fully aware of the depth of your emotions.

It is that heightened state of clarity that gives you the freedom to consciously choose whether to resist, blame, or hold onto the emotion you are experiencing. This can only be so because a healthy mind is connected with the reservoir of acceptance, love, and peace that is your intrinsic nature, your Self.

And you don't need to be a monk in saffron robes, or a nun or saint. You can even be a politician and understand that your heart can be in peace even in the worse of adversity. President Barack Obama understood this very well when he visited the graves of children massacred in a mass shooting and said, "Our hearts are broken by their sudden passing.

Our hearts are broken and yet our hearts also have reasons for fullness."

The key to developing a healthy mind is to train it so well that it becomes available at all times. Train it so well that it can be called up on demand not only when the world is friendly to you but also when it seems to be conspiring against you.

Getting to Know Your Mind

Before you start to train your mind, let's look inward at it. Let's see what the mind looks like and what it does all day long.

Let's shine a light inward to see what we find there right now. Let's do it together.

Set a timer for one minute.

Close your eyes and for one full minute observe what is happening in your mind. Don't judge what you find in your mind as good or bad in any way. Just observe what is happening in your mind. See what is there.

When the minute is over, open your eyes.

What did you see? What was happening in your mind?

If you're like most of us, especially if this is your first time observing your mind, you might be amazed at what is going on in there, at the flood of all kinds of thoughts coming in and out, appearing for a moment and then disappearing, some weak in the background and some strong in the foreground of your attention, a few emotions at a distance pushing to become stronger. A few of the thoughts are recognizable because they are a constant; some are new and trivial; some are not even fully formed. The only consistent theme is the relentless traffic of thoughts, the noise of your thoughts, the nonstop chatter of mostly weird, often negative, uninteresting thoughts. In other words, junk thoughts.

Now you have an inkling of the turbulence of your mind left unchecked. Welcome to the unbridled mind! It's all noise!

Our minds are filled with dysfunctional chatter that goes on twenty-four hours a day, seven days a week. Isn't it shocking that we live our lives with all this mental commotion all the time? Isn't it disturbing that we make life-impacting decisions with all this background noise? Through all this noise we try to understand why we feel what we feel, why we're in the mood we're in, or why we're in the life situation we find ourselves in right now. How clear or stable can our analyses and subsequent choices be in all this racket?

No wonder we look to the outside world for answers: looking inward is just too chaotic, and usually not very helpful. As cleverly put by ABC News anchor Dan Harris in his book *10% Happier*: "The voice in my head is an asshole."

The fact that you're reading *Happiness no Matter What!* leads me to believe that you're not entirely thrilled with where the voice in your head has led you either.

This type of chaotic mind bears little resemblance to the healthy mind that the monk Ricard describes. I hope you're starting to see that the only way to change your life is to change the health of your mind.

The good news is that changing or improving the health of your mind is not only possible but actually quite easy with the right training.

Why Awareness Is Important

First, let's understand what *awareness* is. The term relates loosely to the capacity to pay attention to an event. But it implies much more than the usual untrained way in which you pay attention. Awareness describes a state of mind that fully grasps the experience of your attention. And it does so without the bias of your judgment.

Although it can't be measured, awareness is the basic cognitive quality of the mind. It is what allows you to experience love and compassion. It is through awareness that you grasp the experiences of life. Its quality determines the colors of your life.

The experience of being aware is as profound as that of being mindful. They both describe a way of paying attention that connects you deeply with the present, with what you are living now, with what your experience is right now. If you aren't aware or mindful of what is happening inside or outside you, you can't experience the full richness of life. Life passes you by.

Suppose that you're at the park with your baby and you're not paying attention to what the baby is doing because you're busy texting. You have your baby in your peripheral view, but you're certainly not paying high quality attention, you're not fully present in the moment. That's why you're not aware when your baby starts walking, taking her first steps all by herself. You miss the experience of your heart being filled with awe and happiness at your baby's first steps. You're paying limited attention; you're not fully in the experience of your attention. You're not aware of the moment as it is unfolding.

How many times do we say, "I saw it happening but didn't really see it; otherwise I would have done something about it." Without awareness you can see but you can't fully comprehend the experience of the moment, and so you miss big chunks of life.

We in our Western industrialized societies are not trained in awareness or taught how to pay attention to what is there in the moment. Our minds are bombarded by the noise of all kinds of unsolicited information that filters and interferes with the quality of our experience as we live it. *As a consequence, even our most cherished moments get diluted by our "all over the place" quality of attention.*

Yet if you realize the importance of being present, of living with more awareness, you will want to develop the quality of your attention. You will want to train yourself to become more mindful of what you're doing in every moment, of what your thoughts are, of how you feel, and of what you want to bring into your life. In this first Principle you will start by training your awareness muscles so you can embrace the whole richness of a fully lived life.

Meditation is the basic tool you will be using in this program. It is the most efficient way to start training your mind to pay attention, to become aware, to—in the end—live a fuller life.

Meditation: the Most Powerful Technique for Training Your Awareness Muscles

Although meditation has become almost trendy in the United States, there are still big misconceptions about what meditation really is. It is still shrouded in mystery and connotations of monks in faraway caves, New Age wishful thinkers, or saffron-robed people chanting in public parks. It is also frequently misjudged as an escape mechanism used by people who don't want to face reality, almost like a drug.

Yet meditation is simply a tool for quieting the mind. Yes, sages and monks of all Eastern spiritual traditions and major Western religions have meditated for thousands of years, but meditation does not need to be practiced in a religious context. It stands by itself as a technique.

There are many important and varied kinds of meditation. I teach and practice a meditation style that strengthens the "muscles" of the mind to become more and more aware. It is a technique to quiet the mind, to pay attention to what the mind is doing at any given moment, and to progressively relax it into its own quiet natural state of peace and happiness. This is the style of meditation that you will learn and develop here in the program.

Meditation is a very uncomplicated, effortless technique that, when you learn to practice it correctly and make it part of your daily routine, is profoundly transformational. I have included detailed meditation instructions at the end of the chapter.

Let's look at the basics of meditation. They are simple: You choose an object on which to focus your attention, meaning that you decide what you are going to pay attention to. The chosen object of your attention can be a word or a group of words (also called by the Sanskrit name, *mantra*) that you will mentally repeat. It can also be the breath that you will watch as it goes in and out of the nostrils. What you choose to focus on does not matter. What matters is that you choose one thing to focus on and stick with it, mentally repeating it for the duration of your meditation, until the time is up.

It is important to notice that meditation is a practice and as a practice it needs to be done repeatedly and consistently.

Meditating is as simple a technique as watching your breath or repeating a word, but it can also be difficult—even very difficult. But that difficulty is not inherent to meditation. It can be difficult if you don't follow clear instructions on how to do it, and then get frustrated and uncomfortable. It can also be difficult if you are not patient with yourself and the practice and if you expect instantaneous results. And it can be VERY difficult if you bring expectations of what is supposed to happen while you are meditating, distorting the purpose of your meditation and making it quite annoying.

Please, spend a bit of time becoming familiar with the instructions on how to meditate, at the end of this chapter. Don't improvise or change anything. Just follow the instructions as they are explained. Give it a try!

Living with the newly acquired awareness

After a few weeks of practicing your daily meditation, you will notice changes in you and in your life. They may be very subtle changes, but they are definitely transformational.

1. You become less judgmental.

One of the most important attitudes you bring to your meditation practice is the quality of non-judgment. In the instructions to the breath meditation (at the end of this chapter) that you just practiced, you were guided to see and notice what goes on in your mind as you meditated "without judgment," to just "notice when your mind wanders away and without judging yourself go back to the breath." This way of practicing will strengthen your mind's ability to see and note what is going on in your mind without forcing anything. You will start noticing what you are thinking, what your thoughts are without commentary.

Judging everything at all times is what the untrained mind does, and that is exhausting! Training your mind to pay attention and observe without judgment frees up a lot of your mind space and allows you to see the experience for what it is. The result is a more focused and clear state of mind from which to make decisions.

The more you practice paying attention to your thoughts for what they are, the more you bring that quality of mind to your active life and become much more connected with it.

This way of looking at your thoughts or at what is happening in the moment to you or your life does not mean that you will have no opinions and that you are going to become a total bore, sitting on a couch with a half smile of permanent agreement. As we will see in the Fourth Principle, what it does mean is that your opinions will be based on clear observation of the facts and they will be sharper and more focused than ever, rendering them more interesting and valuable. You will be addressing issues with a clear perception of what they are and what they mean to you and not from your value judgment of them. As a result, you become a much more interesting person that can contribute to the conversation with the sharp edges of true observation.

2. You realize you have options and choices.

As this practice strengthens your awareness of the moment, you become more active and reflective and less reactive and reflexive in your everyday interactions.

Suppose you are at the grocery store and a man coming down the aisle pushes past you and is openly rude and a bit confrontational. Your habitual knee-jerk reaction might be to call this person rude and for your voice to become louder so that everybody can hear how awful this man is and take your side in the confrontation. You ask the man for an apology and the situation becomes really heated. You are now at the height of your anger and indignation, you are red in the face, you are sweating and you demand to talk to the manager... I am sure you can easily imagine the scene. It is not an unusual event. We have all been witnesses to similar ones at the store, at the office, at the bus, and even at home.

On the other hand, if you had been meditating for a while, your attitude to the event and to the man would probably be quite different. The man's rudeness might spark a hint of anger or annoyance in you and maybe even the urge to engage with him in anger, but you would catch your feelings as they start to bubble up, and that second of awareness would give you the space and clarity from which to choose the best course of action for you and everybody else in the situation. I am quite sure that you would just let it go and move on with your shopping.

3. *You live your life more fully. You become engaged with the richness of life.*

As you begin to train your awareness, you notice more and more what your thoughts are, the quality of your thoughts, and what you are paying attention to in the moment and more generally in your life. You will catch yourself noticing a beautiful sunset and you will put away your smart phone to enjoy it. You will notice that you are starting to actually listen to what people are saying instead of pretending to listen to them. You will realize that there is a bird singing at your window sill and you will enjoy the gift of its music. You will catch a useless negative thought and change it into a more life-affirming one. You will find that those experiential nuggets will begin to add vibrancy to your life, making it richer, more meaningful, and happier.

Why would you want to quiet your mind? Why is it necessary?

Silence is the backdrop of a clear and focused mind. It is the inherent quality of your mind behind the turmoil of your thoughts.

Ancient sages, seers, and monks knew about the benefits of a quiet mind but they did not exalt silence for the sake of silence. They sought silence as the necessary condition for heightening their awareness. To be able to see their thoughts as separate from their own true essence, just as little spirals of energy in the mind and nothing else. They knew that the progressive quieting of the mind would take their mind to expanded states of awareness, leading to engaging with life in a more meaningful way. They also knew that it is in that silence that you meet your Self, your natural state of peace and happiness.

Thus, as you spend time with your Self in meditation, you get immersed in your Self's attributes of wisdom, creativity, wholeness, stillness, compassion, and kindness, what the Buddhists call the "luminous aspect of the mind." This quality permeates your active life outside of your meditation practice.

In other words, every time you meditate, you dip into this transformational state of being that can only happen when there is quiet and stillness in the mind.

But if you want to transform, you don't even need to accept or know any of these claims extracted from all the wisdom traditions. What you have to do, though, is to practice meditation and become the witness and owner of your mind.

How do you know if meditation is working for you?

Here are two of the most common side effects of your practice:

1. Others will notice changes you might not be aware of.

If you have been meditating for a few weeks, and you don't notice any changes and don't think your practice is working, don't be discouraged; the people around you will indeed detect your change. Your co-workers, your family, your friends will see changes in the way you look or smile, but most often they will be surprised by changes in the way you deal with situations.

Some will be confused and disconcerted because what they expect from you is not happening anymore. Some others will be pleasantly surprised but attribute this change to a vacation, better relationship, a salary raise, etc.

For example, when your teenage son gives you the "yeah rrrright" smile that he knows drives you crazy, you will not immediately react the same way you have always reacted—screaming, lecturing, menacing, or whatever else you usually do. You will instead notice the smirk on his face with a bit of spaciousness, of distance, with no thought, with an awareness that will let you see the situation for what it is. This second of clarity will allow you to decide whether to yell at him, giving in to his provocation as is your habitual reaction, or to explain to him with calmness and truth why that smile is so annoying to you, or whatever else feels appropriate to you. The point is that regardless of what you choose to do or say, it will be your decision and choice, and not your usual knee jerk reaction. Your interaction with him will come from a place of spaciousness and clarity, and he will notice that! After this happens a few times, before you leave the room, turn around and look at your son's face, mildly intrigued and quite confused; he has noticed...

2. You will realize that your emotions are not taking you for granted.

As you practice applying the filter of clarity to your mind, you become quite adept at noticing not only what is happening outside yourself but, most importantly, what is happening inside your mind and your body. You start to catch your thoughts the moment they appear, and in time you will be able to see when they begin to turn into sensations about to spiral into emotions of exasperation, sadness, anger, disillusion, hate, despair—the whole spectrum of our daily melodramas.

You will also notice when your mind and body contract in resistance to what is happening, when you oppose the experience you are dealing with. With that clarity, you can choose either to hang onto that resistance or to let it go.

You will definitely notice how living with more clarity frees your mind and body of the baggage of useless, fierce, uncontrolled emotions, and how this results in a much more peaceful and pleasurable life.

Practice, and commitment to more practice, is the only way.

Meditation is not a hobby, an activity or exercise that you do every now and then. If you look at it as a hobby, you'd do better to collect stamps or porcelain dolls. But if you really want to transform yourself into happiness, you have to make a daily commitment to the practice and you have to be patient. In the same way that you cannot expect to develop your triceps by going to the gym once or twice a month, without discipline, commitment, and patience, you cannot expect to train your mind into the silence of meditation. It does not work that way.

If you are serious about changing your life into one that is happier and more fulfilled, you have to commit to the practice of meditation with determination and you have to give it daily time. It has to become a welcome ritual in your daily life.

Transformation is guaranteed—but it does not come overnight.

The effects of your meditation practice do not happen overnight, but they do not take forever either.

In only a few weeks you will start to see changes. And that is great news! You don't need to spend years in meditation to see changes in yourself or your life, or even many months. This is a fact supported by findings of scientific studies on the physiological effects of meditation. One of the most striking findings is that after only eight weeks of meditation, structures in the brain associated with aggression and stress—mostly the amygdala—change. The amygdala shrinks!

Think about this: if only eight weeks of practicing meditation can change structures in your brain, what could a year or eight years of the practice do for you?

The new science of neuroplasticity has gone even further and shown that the atrophy produced in the neurons by aging diminishes considerably, and sometimes even disappears completely, after a few months of practicing meditation. If this is not enough of an argument to have you commit to giving the practice a chance, Deepak Chopra and Rudy Tanzy just published a book with the results of their research showing that where you put your attention and how you think can alter the behavior of up to 90% of your genes.

Given these findings, do you really want to allow your attention to wander into empty, dysfunctional, unproductive thoughts, or do you want to consciously light up your happy, creative genes?

The Two Biggest Obstacles to Practicing Meditation

1. You believe that your thoughts are your meditation enemies.

There is a widespread misconception that when you sit down to meditate, you order your mind to be quiet and your thoughts disappear. Regardless of how many times you have been told that thoughts are part of the "practice" you mostly don't think this is true, not your truth anyway. If you are going to spend the time, you want to make sure it is well spent and so you decide that if you are "good at it," you will have no thoughts. After a few days or weeks or even months of chasing your thoughts, hyperventilating, and getting annoyed and frustrated, you declare, "Meditation is not for me," and you stop.

But actually, thoughts are not your meditation enemies, they are your meditation friends. If you did not have thoughts, you would not need to meditate.

Please, go back to the meditation instructions and you will notice that at no point do they instruct you to quiet your thoughts. Nowhere are you told to watch your breath for 15 or 20 minutes straight without having thoughts. You will not and you cannot because you are human. I don't think the Dalai Lama, Deepak Chopra, or even ever-present-in-the-now Eckhart Tolle can be without thoughts for more than a few minutes at most—and on a good day. The point is that chasing your thoughts is not meditation. Noticing your thoughts and going back to your object of attention is the practice that trains your attention and takes you into stillness.

At the beginning of your meditation practice you will have thoughts most of the time. At some point, though, you will become keenly aware of them, look at them, and be able to choose to let them go. Little by little, you will have a few intervals of less and less thought and, eventually, little gaps of stillness and silence in between thoughts. But you don't force anything, you don't chase or pursue or expect anything; you just let the process unfold by itself.

2. Expectations of any kind hamper the practice.

As we already noted above, expectations on what is supposed to happen make a sustainable meditation practice very difficult. Many times, newcomers to meditation expect to have amazing, spectacular experiences, some straight out of science fiction movies, to more modest ones of out-of-body experiences, visions of colors and music, meetings with spiritual guides and angels, and travel to lands and scenes from other worlds.

It is not unusual to have a few of those experiences as you first begin to meditate, or you may read about them in books, so that every time you sit to meditate you bring that expectation to the practice. You expect or hope to have these "otherworldly" experiences. When they do not materialize, you think that you are doing something wrong and you feel disappointed, and you probably stop meditating altogether.

I don't know why these surreal experiences happen, but I do know that we do not meditate simply to have those experiences. If there are fireworks on the road to quiet, it may be fun and interesting, but they are not the object of your meditation. Those fireworks can be a deterrent and a detriment to the practice, because they are distracting you from your objectives to quiet the mind and to look without judgment.

If you have these kinds of experiences while you are meditating, train your mind to just look at them, notice them without judgment, and let them go. Go back to watching your breath.

There is only one kind of bad meditation: The one you do not do, the one you skip, the one you do not show up for.

COMMIT AND LET IT HAPPEN!
Let the road to your happiness be clear.

♋

The ultimate value of life depends upon awareness and the power of contemplation rather than upon mere survival.

- Aristotle

Meditation Instructions

Breath Meditation

1. Choose a place as quiet as possible and where you will not be disturbed. Preferably, dim the lights a bit, just gentle reading light, but avoid total darkness.

2. Silence your phone. I recommend airplane mode with the wireless off so texts don't come through and you can still use your timer. Set the timer for 10 or 15 minutes, ideally 20.

3. Sit comfortably, on a chair or on a cushion on the floor. Make sure that your back is straight but not rigid. Your palms are resting on your thighs. If you are sitting on a chair, your feet should be planted on the floor. Make sure you do not slouch. You might want to use some lower back support. The key here is to find a position that you are willing to commit to for the duration of your meditation without inviting you to sleep.

4. Close your eyes, take a few deep breaths, slow, long, and relaxed. Take a moment to notice the noises in the room and the smells in the room. Feel your body as it rests on the chair. Notice all sensations outside and inside your body. Do not look for them, do not dwell on them, just notice them as they come up and gently let them go. Some will not leave easily (like an itch or an ache), but continue to notice them and then let them go again. Gently, do not force anything.

5. Now focus your attention on the sensation of your breath at your nostrils, how it comes in and how it goes out. Just watch it. Don't force it, don't follow your breath, just notice it as it comes in and out again and again. It is a very gentle process of noticing without any judgment. Just let it happen and observe, witness it.

6. As your mind wanders away from your breath—which will happen—notice where it has gone, and gently bring your attention back to your breath. Just let the thought go and return to your breath.

7. When physical sensations, noises in the room, or emotions take you away from the breath—which will happen—and you notice it, gently bring your attention back to your breath.

8. When your attention drifts away and you are lost in thought, daydreaming, miles away from your chair— which will happen—notice it, look at your daydream, and gently let it go. Go back to noticing your breath at your nostrils, in and out.

9. When the voice in your head starts telling you that you are doing it all wrong, that you are a loser, that you cannot even meditate—which will happen—notice the voice and gently go back to your breathing.

10. When your back starts to hurt and your knee starts to ache, don't be tempted to change positions. Today you

committed to this seat, tomorrow you can pick another. Notice the discomfort and, unless it is excruciating, choose to go back to your breath. If it continues to be uncomfortable, choose to change position with mindfulness of what you are doing and go back to your breath.

11. Do this process of losing your attention again and again and gently bringing it back to your breath again and again, without judgment. You are not failing. This is how you meditate, how you practice the muscle of your attention to stay focused where you want it to focus: on your breath. Repeat the process again and again. Keep the process going until the alarm goes off.

12. When the alarm goes off, take a slow deep breath, keep your eyes closed, stop focusing on the breath, and just sit there for a moment in total silence without a thought.

13. When you are ready, open your eyes and smile at your Self. You are meditating—you are doing something great for yourself!

You will find Mantra Meditation Instructions in the Appendix at the end of the book.

If you would like to practice with guided meditations, I have a few that my clients find very helpful. Go to my website, www.monicabelizan.com, and click on the meditations icon.

Working the Principle

Training My Mind to Pay Attention

My awareness determines the quality of my life.

This week's practices will lead you to build your meditation practice and show you how to meditate in a relaxed way so that you become comfortable with your new meditation practice and you keep it for life. They will lead you to heightened awareness and therefore clarity and focus.

EXERCISES

1. I will meditate everyday morning and evening.

Become familiar with the Meditation Instructions just before this section and practice the breath meditation twice a day. (Alternatively, if you prefer, you can practice the mantra meditation—instructions in the Appendix at the end of the book.)

If you feel comfortable meditating for 20 minutes each time, that will be optimal. If not, start with just 10 minutes for the first week and then increase the meditation time by an extra minute or two each week until you get to 20 minutes each time. A few minutes every day are more important than meditating for a long time every now and then.

If you skip a day, just come back to your practice the next day. Be kind to yourself, no judgment, simply go back to your practice.

Congratulate yourself! You are starting a practice that will help you become a better version of yourself than you ever thought possible. You are gaining clarity, focus, and the freedom to choose the way you live.

2. *Several times a day I will stop what I am doing to pay deliberate attention to what it really is that I am doing and how I am doing it.*

I will ask myself,

What am I doing right now?
Why am I doing it right now?
How am I doing it right now?

Look at your answers as indicators of how connected you are with what you are doing, thinking, or feeling at any time. If you realize you are not paying attention and are disconnected, take a deep breath and decide to pay attention to the moment as it is.

The idea is not to judge yourself but to be mindful of where your thoughts are and how they relate to what you are experiencing. You are training your mind to pay attention to what you're doing.

Set up a reminder in your phone to buzz you once every hour.

3. *Several times a day I'll pay deliberate undivided attention to what somebody's saying to me, in person, by phone, or by text message. I'll refrain from saying anything until the person is finished talking. When my attention wanders away from the conversation, I'll bring it back to it again and again.*

Set up reminders of mindful listening with sticky notes on your phone, computer, and elsewhere at home, the office, and other places where you most interact with family, friends, and co-workers.

SECOND PRINCIPLE

Knowing Who You Are
You're so much more than you think you are.

Knowing others is wisdom, knowing yourself is enlightenment.

- Lao Tzu

Knowing who we truly are is the most important piece of information we can possibly have. Only when we know who we are, can we know what to expect and demand of ourselves. Only when we know who we are can we know how to treat ourselves and others. Only when we know who we are can we be joyful participants of life in all its richness.

Yet, if I walk into a room with 500 people and ask: Who are you? I will most likely have 499 people tell me who they are not. The one exception will probably be someone asleep, or worse yet, checking emails.

You are probably thinking that this is a dumb question. Who am I? Of course I know who I am. I am this person who wakes up in the morning and drinks coffee, spends eight to ten or maybe twenty hours a day at the office doing things to earn a salary. I have kids and every now and then I go on a vacation. Oh, and I live in Chicago although I was born in South Africa...

But is that who you really are at the end of the day? Are you your job? Your profession? Your success? Your lack of success? Your excitement or your boredom at work? Your nationality? Is that who you truly are? I don't think so. You are not a name, an age, a nationality, a teacher, a father. You are not the one who works as a doctor or nurse, carpenter or baker. Those are your experiences along your walk through life on planet earth. But that is not your essence, your core; that is not who you really, really are.

So if you are not what you do or what your family or your place in society says about you, who are you?

Are you your thoughts?

Although we completely identify with the voice in our heads and the thoughts it tells us, we are not our thoughts. The constant voice in your head is mostly churning around what your senses have told it about the world and yourself, plus your memories, feelings, emotions, and beliefs. And although the mind is a powerful tool to cherish and important to cultivate, it is not telling you the whole picture of who you are.

You are the Being that thinks the thoughts. You are the Self that knows your mind but lies beyond it.

The idea that we are our thoughts is a very common and disruptive assumption in our Western world. We mostly owe its popularity to the French philosopher René Descartes's famous statement, "I think therefore I am." In all reality he should have said, "I Am therefore I can think, too." As Eckhart Tolle says, it took three hundred years until Jean Paul Sartre realized that the consciousness that says "I am" is not the same consciousness that thinks. In other words, when you are aware that you are thinking, you are separate from your thoughts. So how can you just be your thoughts?

You can be alive and have no thoughts, as if in deep relaxation. You can keep your mind so still that you have no thoughts, like a monk in the Himalayas meditating weeks at the time, but you are very much alive. You are that which is behind the thoughts.

Davidji, one of the most inspiring teachers at the Chopra Center, used to say (and I paraphrase him here): "If you think you are your thoughts, tell me what you are thinking right now. Are you thinking about the dinner you will have soon? Are you your dinner? No. You are a whole human being thinking about it."

You are the one who is doing the process of thinking and watching the process of thinking; you are the witness.

If you cannot feel or identify with your Being just yet, don't worry. You will as you stick to your daily meditation and practice the Principles of this program. In time you will begin to experience your Being.

Are you your body?

Your body is an amazingly sophisticated piece of machinery, but it is not who you are either. Many religions consider the human body the sacred temple of the soul, but the temple provides only temporary housing. Once the temple disintegrates, the soul moves on into other dimensions.

Children are the first to know that life continues after the body is dead. It is not uncommon for children to see and talk to a grandparent who has recently died. They say that they see the grandparent, and it does not mean that they are lying or imagining it. They can do it because the blinds of conditioning—of who they are and what they should expect from themselves—have not been completely drawn for them. For the first years of their lives they remain connected with their true Self and its multiple dimensions and they can truly see their deceased grandparent.

As we grow up, we lose that connection to our true Self. We shrink from our larger potential. We learn to ignore the tremendous depth of who we are. We end up with a reductionist view of who we are even when the truth of our Self keeps seeping into our awareness, sometimes so spectacularly so that it makes the news!

For instance, a few years ago it was all over the news: the "amazing" story about a woman who lifted a car with one hand in order to rescue her child from under that car. Where did she get that strength from? In that moment, her state of mind was such that she was not limited by her beliefs in what she was capable of doing or achieving. Her desperation freed her from the limitations of her body-mind beliefs, and because of that she was able to reach a force in a dimension beyond her physical, everyday existence. She contacted the field of pure awareness, where all possibilities exist. She immersed herself in the domain of her real Self and from the limitless unbounded dimension of her Self, she could do the impossible. She did what she could not have done with her small self, her ego self.

We have seen many of these intriguing events reported in the news, but we are so limited by what we want to believe is our reality, we don't get the full meaning and implications of these apparently unexplainable events.

In a less spectacular way we all have these instances of what we call "miracles" in our everyday life. Think of the time when you did something that, looking back, you said "I don't know how I did it, I had no idea of it while doing it"—from finding an address without previous knowledge to successfully baking a cake without the recipe to passing an exam with great grades although you thought you did not know enough to knowing exactly what your friend needs to make her feel better.

Everyday events that you attribute to help from the angels, good luck, chance, or a miracle, happen mostly when your powerful Self slips through your ego, intellect and mind, and your greatness can shine through.

It is interesting that we feel more comfortable with the idea that we are much less than we really are than with the possibility that we might indeed be truly powerful. We owe it to ourselves to start accepting that we are much more than bones, flesh, thoughts, and intellect.

Are you your ego?

To get to the root of why we limit ourselves to believing we are just our body and mind cloaked in our small self, we have to meet our ego and realize the huge, all-pervasive role it plays in who we think we are and how we live our lives.

Ego is a psychological structure that we build slowly but surely from early childhood. It is a gimmick that, if left unbridled, becomes who we think we are and ends up running our lives.

We come into this world imbued with the essence of pure uncompromising love. Love is our nature and the world our physical extension. We are thrilled giving and receiving love and cry over its absence. We have no fear. Love, trust, and happiness are our nature. But this angelic state of bountiful love does not last long.

Eckhart Tolle finds the very first element of ego construction very early in our lives, when we are introduced to the word "I." With that word we start to develop the idea of who we are. We identify with the idea of "I" and soon with "me" and "mine," thus my toys, parents, teachers, and everything that touches me becomes part of "I." That's why we as children feel very threatened when these objects of identification disappear or are broken.

Growing up and adapting to family, friends, school, and society in general becomes a serious process of identification with what is acceptable and required. Fear creeps in—what if I don't have what it takes to be accepted. What if I am rejected?

Your teenage years are mainly a struggle and race to identify with gender, possessions, roles, looks, nationality, opinions, memories, and emotions. Collections of thoughts that you string together so strongly by your identification with them that they become your ego personality, a mask you create to hide your fears. Little by little, you successfully peel off the layers of your connection to your Self and replace them with bands of alliance to your ego mask. And you think this mask is who you really are.

It is as if you put a suit on to go out and you end up thinking you are the suit!

It is not the intention of this book to destroy the ego but unveil its role in our lives and to realize the power it has on who we think we really are.

How do you know if you are driven by your ego or your Self?

Fear keeps the ego strong and shapes who you think you are, what you do, what you like, who you like, who you don't like. When you come from ego, fear is behind every decision you make.

Maybe at one point or another in your life you felt that you wanted something different, better, more motivating, rewarding, happier, or had the urge to change careers, follow your dreams, leave a negative relationship, move to a new country or city. And then you stopped to listen to what you "know" from experience, yours or that of your parents, friends, and society. You listened to the voice in your head saying: it is going to cost money you don't have, you are too old, too young, you don't know enough, you cannot believe what you don't see, dreaming is impractical, wait until you are 100% sure—and all such kinds of defeatist propositions. The voice in your head managed to cramp your insipient desire with fears of failure, doom, and disaster, and you ended up disavowing your desire. It stopped you in your tracks.

If that ever happened to you, know that it was your ego at work.

If you want to know the voice of the ego, every time you are about to make a decision, ask yourself, "Is this voice in my head coming from fear or from trust and happiness?" If the voice is rife with tones of scarcity, negativity, and darkness, know that the ego is talking and making sure you stay within known limits.

So what do you call who you really are?

The answer will differ, depending on your spiritual, religious, cultural, and/or philosophical tendencies. God, divinity, soul, Self, Christ, Jesus, Universe, love, light, Brahma, Jesus, Muhammad, Buddha, Tao, Shiva, Yahweh, and Spirit are some of the more common names given to who we really, really are, and I agree with all of them. They all point to the same truth, and not one is better than another in describing your and my intrinsic natures as powerful and unlimited.

I choose to call my essence Self or Being. A particular instance or manifestation of the Source from which I, you, and everything else come into existence. It is divine in that it never dies, immensely creative, and abundant. It is love and its domain is the field of infinite possibilities. And we all share this same essence with everybody else on this planet. Only our external form is different, in the same way every single wave in the ocean is different from all others but they all share the same inherent "oceanic" quality.

You may be uncomfortable with such terms as godlike, divine, light, and love to describe your essence—and that is perfectly fine. You might choose instead to look at what science has to say on the nature of your human essence.

David Bohm, one of the founding fathers of quantum physics, illustrated the workings of a unified, undivided cosmos by saying that the universe works like a grand cosmic hologram. In a hologram, every portion of an object contains that object in its entirety, only on a smaller scale. Max Planck, the father of quantum theory, said that there is a matrix where the birth of stars, the DNA of life, and everything in between originates. Gregg Braden, scientist and best-selling New Age literature author, calls it the Divine Matrix.

It seems to me that they are talking about what the ancient scriptures of every major religion in the world already knew: there is a Source from where we come and we are all part of it and we always stay connected to it. Maybe the name is Matrix, or God, or Self, Source, or Spirit. It is not important what we name it

So take your pick of what you want to call that core essence that is you. And if you have a good name for it, one that resonates more with you, use it instead of the one I suggest. The naming is not important to the process of discovery and transformation.

What is profoundly important is that you know that there is so much more to who you think you are. That your authentic "I" has nothing to do with the ego and its limiting beliefs or with what the outside world has been telling you that you are. *Claim your inheritance!*

You owe it to yourself to open up and enjoy the riches of your Self.

Jesus said, "Be still and know you are God."

The Buddha said, "If you see the Buddha down the road kill him." (You are your own Buddha).

Vedanta says, "Man, nature, and god are all the same."

How do you go beyond living from your ego to living from your authentic Self?

Knowing who you are cannot be learned from teachers and theory only; you have to have the experience of your Self. As you deepen your meditation practice you will spend more and more time in the silence of your mind where you find your Self. Little by little you will start to recognize when you are aligned with your Self and when you are not.

This Essential Seven Principles Program is indeed an invitation to enter a path that takes you to your real Self. As you continue to study and practice each of the Principles, you will start entering the chambers of your full, immense potential. As you deepen your alignment with your true Self you will fly higher than you ever thought possible.

The practices specific for this week are designed so that you can consciously incorporate who you truly are and your boundless potential into your mind and life. In time you will be more and more aware of the spaciousness that being present in stillnes brings into your life. You will experience Self and become more familiar with it, you and your life will transform while your ego withers away.

♋

What lies behind us and what lies before us are
tiny matters compared to what lies within us.

\- Ralph Waldo Emerson

Working the Principle

My True Self Is Magnificent!

Feeling my essence

This week's practices will help you start peeling back layers of conditioning to allow the essence of your amazing Self to shine through.

EXERCISES

1. *Just as I close my eyes at the beginning of my morning and evening meditations I will ask my Self:*

> *Who am I?*
> *Who am I?*
> *Who am I?*

Don't expect or speculate on any answer. Just ask and trust the process. You are dropping your question in the silence of your Self. In the same way that you would drop a seed in fertile soil, know that it will sprout, grow and give you answers.

Remember: Being is not found by thinking it, but in the silent experience.

2. I will feel my inner body. Feeling it will help me see that I'm not just this body and mind I think I am. I'll experience my life energy, my essence, my Self.

Sit down with your eyes closed.

Bring your attention to the palms of your hands and "feel" them. Give it a little bit of time until you feel an aliveness in them.

Now move your attention to your feet; keep it there till you again feel the inner energy. Allow your attention to feel hands and feet at the same time.

Gently bring your attention to your chest, lower back, legs, arms.

Stay very still with the inner experience, until you become aware of an inner-body sense of aliveness.

After a few moments open your eyes.

In time it will become easy and you will be able to get into the inner body on command. You are moving away from identifying with your body to experiencing your Self. [1]

3. I will make a daily commitment to stop to look at things that I like.

Every day take a moment to look at a flower, a drop of water, a cloud, a baby, a puppy. Just look at it in silence without any judgment, without any verbal or mental commentary.

---

[1] This is an exercise that I learned from Echart Tolle. He calls it your essence identity. He says that this body-awareness exercise even strengthens the immune system! You can read more about it in his book *The Power of Now*, page 53.

Allow yourself to be with the flower, or whatever you choose, and sense it, observe it without judgment, notice how you feel. Experience how beauty reveals itself in the moment, how it sprouts from your essence and reaches out, merging with that flower. Feel the beauty and peace of your Self communing with the flower.

4. When making a decision I will stop to ask myself:

> *Am I deciding from my Self or from my ego?*
> *Is this the voice of Spirit, Love, and Trust,*
> *or is it the voice of the ego?*
> *Is it shrouded by fear and mistrust or by light and hope?*

When asking the questions of your Self, check for body clues. See if the heart area or abdomen are soft and relaxed or if you can feel tightness and constriction.

Remember: Set up sticky notes as reminders of these practices on your phone, purse, desk, kitchen, and places you use frequently.

THIRD PRINCIPLE

Loving Myself—As If I Were My Best Friend

I wish I could treat myself the way my GPS treats me.

You yourself, as much as anybody in the entire universe, deserve your love and affection.

- Buddha

For a long time and ever since I was very young, I was intrigued by the idea of loving myself. I had heard about it many times and I pondered it, but it never made much sense to me. I thought that loving myself was a kind of skill that I had to acquire, like learning to write with the left hand although I was right-handed, or that it meant something I could do only after I owned attributes that could validate the reasons for loving myself, such as being very smart, perfect, rich, popular, gorgeous, and maybe even famous.

I ended up accepting that I did not qualify as any of those charismatic attributes that would make me love myself. I was no Mother Teresa, Einstein, or movie star.

But I remained intrigued about the whole concept, so later on in my life I decided to ask my friends and people I knew about it, and I ran my own self-love poll. I wanted to see what they thought about it and if they had any clues about how to love oneself.

So I asked almost everybody I knew one at a time: "Do you love yourself?" I was shocked that no one said yes or seemed to know what I was referring to. They were all surprised and uncomfortable with the question. Some even thought it was a trick to make them look silly. They had no idea what it meant.

They were quick to tell me, though, who they loved: their parents, their friends, and maybe a teacher or a sibling. But they could not relate to the experience of loving themselves.

I realized then that no one teaches you how to love yourself. Not because people are keeping the wisdom to themselves and don't want to share it, but because most of us talk about self-love but we don't know what it is or how to go about it.

My conclusion was that self-love seemed to be a particular way of feeling towards ourselves that most people don't care to think about. We don't care either because we all love ourselves so much that talking or learning about it would be redundant or because we have no idea what it means and how important it is to love ourselves. We all have felt how love for others feels: wonderful! But wouldn't it be equally wonderful to feel how love for you—by you—feels?

In this Principle you will learn what it means to love yourself and you will practice ways of loving yourself until you incorporate them in your body and mind unconditionally.

What Self-Love Is—What it Is Not

Self-esteem is not self-love.

As much as self-love does not seem to score high in the pursuit of wellness, self-esteem has everybody trying to get as much of it as they possibly can.

Self-esteem is a judgment of oneself, of your own worth. The proponents of self-esteem as a measure of success suggest that in order to have good self-esteem you have to believe and feel you are indeed very successful. And the way you get there is by measuring yourself against everybody else, by being better than or superior to everybody else. It has gotten so out of hand that you cannot be average or "common" anymore. To be considered successful, you have to be exceptional.

Self-esteem is seen as an absolutely necessary ingredient in the formula used by school admissions officers as an indicator of performance. It has become a trusted Human Resources predictor of how you will do in your job. The scale that measures your self-esteem values your aptitude for life: a low grade means that you are a loser with little value, while a healthy, high grade means that you have great value, therefore you are awesome.

Because of the perceived importance of good self-esteem, people work hard to achieve it. This makes sense if you believe that as you raise your self-esteem, you raise your value in your own eyes and in the eyes of those who judge you.

This race to be awesome as fast as possible has been captured by a huge industry that promises to deliver big chunks of self-esteem if you buy whatever it is they are selling. It targets the whole gamut of human existence—cosmetics, plastic surgery, cars, housing, vacations, clothing, restaurants, schools, neighborhoods, even special courses and seminars. They all promise to make you feel better about yourself, to raise your value so that you can compete better in this world. Not even children are spared from learning to be awesome. They play with toys that aim to be role models for the winners in this race, just like Barbie's boyfriend "totally cool Ken" and other manufactured role models.

I find this self-esteem doctrine that emphasizes your worth quite disruptive and damaging. It's a recipe for a life riddled with anxiety and frustration that can easily lead to depression or delusional narcissism.

Another disquieting assumption of the self-esteem judgment underlying the need to be the best at whatever you do is that you are not allowed to make mistakes. You cannot have faults. Faults and mistakes show that you are not awesomely special! So when you do make a mistake or fall short of everybody's expectations, you do not want to admit it, because accepting your mistakes would mean your worth is very little. It can be really devastating.

In our daily life we frequently reinforce this tendency to deny our flaws or mistakes and those of the people we love. If a friend is feeling miserable because he's made a big mistake, your immediate reaction is to help him get over his "failure." As most of us would, you'd probably help him feel good again by bringing up all the things that he does really well and all that he's achieved. You repeat his triumphs again and again until he begins to get out of his misery and starts to agree with you. You and he together manage to restore his grandiose ego until he forgets about his mistake and he can move on to feeling awesome again, almost as good as "totally awesome Ken."

Feeling good about yourself is a healthy attitude to have, and it's important that you cultivate it. Having a good sense of your achievements and your talents and holding a positive and open view of your possibilities is an evolutionary and inspired way of living. But you do not get to that feeling by comparing and measuring your standing against others. You don't value yourself by referring to a comparison chart.

Imperfection is part of being human. You and I and all of us have flaws and make mistakes. When you deny them because you are afraid of failing, of being a failure, you deny yourself the opportunity to work on them in ways that can be more life-enhancing and can contribute to creating an authentically good feeling about yourself.

I hope that soon the whole self-esteem obsession will give way to a better understanding of who we are and what we are made of, of how we deserve to treat ourselves with kindness, of how in kindness to ourselves we can contribute to the betterment of our lives, our societies, and the planet.

But for now, let me assure you that self-esteem is not related to loving yourself.

Self-compassion is an important step in the right direction.

In total contrast to the absurdity of the self-esteem race is the concept of compassion. Compassion is a well-known term, but it is mostly misunderstood and deprived of the richness of its meaning. Some people even get uncomfortable when they hear the word compassion, because they think it is something that cool, "successful" people don't experience, or that it has religious connotations (maybe it is even related to Buddhism, and it would be better if it stayed with the monks in the Himalayan caves).

Simply put, though, compassion is the way you relate to others when you feel connected with them. It describes the way you feel when somebody else is suffering. Because you feel connected with the other person, you want to—and can— help alleviate her suffering.

Self-compassion is the way you relate to yourself when you are connected with your true Self and accept that as a human being you are vulnerable.

You embrace yourself as you are with all your faults, insecurities, defeats, triumphs, skills, and talents. You look at your mistakes or flaws and adjust to the truth of what is happening. You don't judge and compare yourself with anything or anybody else. Your self-worth is not in question. When you make a mistake, you don't feel you are a failure; you instead realize that the mistake hurts and that you don't feel good about it. You may feel frustrated, angry, sad, annoyed, and more, but the feelings are not related to how you value yourself, to your worth. They are related to the experience you just had that probably needs reviewing in order to find the way to a happier outcome.

Practicing self-compassion means that you treat yourself with the same kindness, understanding, and generosity as you treat your friend.

Suppose a friend comes to you distraught and desperate because she didn't get the job promotion she was so hoping to get. As a true friend, you wouldn't judge her as a loser and would certainly not call her a failure, good-for-nothing, pretentious idiot—as you might well call yourself in the same situation. Instead, you would compassionately hold the space for her to feel as rejected and as awful as she wants and needs to. You'd encourage her to feel and notice her pain, anger, or frustration while making sure that she understands that although her expectations have not been met, that doesn't change who she really, really is: a wonderful Self, full of potential. You would not allow or encourage her to judge herself, to diminish her value or the value of anybody else involved. You might even help her see if she can find a weakness in her presentation so as to work on it and be better prepared the next time the possibility of a promotion arises. You can only be this way with her if you are a truly compassionate friend.

Can you honestly say that this is the way you treat yourself when you don't get a promotion or you make a mistake? Most of us cannot say that it is true. It does not come naturally or easily to us, mainly because we are conditioned by the idea of self-esteem. We need to be proud of our excellence, we need to feel we are great, and if we make mistakes and have flaws, instead of compassionately helping ourselves feel less hurt, our prayer and hope is that nobody notices them.

You owe it to yourself to learn to relate to yourself with compassion. Treating yourself kindly is tremendously important if you want happiness in your life. It is urgent—and it can be learned.

In my experience with my clients, I find that they easily accept the concept of compassion as a way to connect with and truly help others, but they do not so readily accept the idea of treating themselves as if they were their own true friend. This idea makes them quite uncomfortable. They think that treating themselves with self-compassion is the surest way to lose their competitive edge, and that embracing their vulnerability will make them complaisant with their flaws and weaknesses, rendering themselves unimportant or inconsequential. In other words, they feel threatened when they connect with their vulnerability.

Self-compassion does not mean that you become a self-gratifying bore and lose interest and ambition for doing great things with your life. What it means is that you do everything from a different perspective. You know who you are and how you are, you look at your skills and flaws, and with kindness you start to work on how to harmonize them in creative ways. You don't judge and you don't hide anything, you just connect with your reality at this very moment, as it is today.

Embracing compassion as a way to relate to yourself involves accepting that you are human and that suffering is part of the whole human experience. You have to admit that you are suffering when you are, and that you're in pain when you're in pain, rather than try to gloss it over or hide it from yourself. *Simply put, suffering is part of our human experience, and compassion acknowledges it as such.*

Compassion knows suffering is human.

We talk about pain and suffering, but most of us think that we don't suffer pain in our daily lives, only in extreme circumstances—if we are terminally ill, lose a loved one, or experience acute physical pain. This is suffering, but it is only one kind of suffering.

There is another kind that we bear most of the time but that we're not aware of. It's an emotional and psychological kind of suffering that affects everybody in our Western world. We suffer all the time because we judge ourselves as not being or having enough of what people value in the world—money, education, health, wisdom—whatever it is we decide we need to have in order to be more, to place us higher on the success scale. Not reaching those standards renders us disempowered and unworthy—and that is a profoundly painful emotional experience. We shut down and become depressed.

If we want to lead lives that are happy and whole, we need to come to terms with our suffering. Not as a "face reality and talk about it" exercise, but as an acknowledgment of the totality of who we are, and that includes our emotions and feelings.

By facing the pain head-on, we can see what is really causing it, and begin to realize that we are suffering not so much because we didn't get that promotion but because of our habit of considering ourselves "less than." When we achieve full awareness of our suffering and its causes, we may still be upset for not fulfilling our expectations, but we will not experience the self-deprecating emotion of worthlessness. Become aware of your pain and begin the healing process of self-compassion.

I love to quote one of my clients who said, "I wish I could treat myself like my GPS treats me. It just points the way and never tells me: I told you to turn left and you didn't, look at where you are now, you cannot follow instructions and now you have no idea of where you are!"

Maybe we should all take lessons from the unconditional, non-judgmental, helpful love of the GPS!

From Self-Compassion to True Self-Love

Understanding and practicing self-compassion is an important step toward living more peacefully and with much more happiness. But I'm going to push you further. I believe that there is still distance to cover between acting like your own best friend and actually loving yourself. Self-compassion brings you close to it, but you're not there yet.

The legendary spiritual teacher and author of the seminal book *Be Here Now*, Ram Dass, says that you are in love when you are in a state of Being. It means the state you are in when you are aligned with the energy of your Self that is pure Love.

Love is your natural state and that is why when you feel it, your whole body and mind vibrate at higher frequencies. You feel it freely flowing through your entire body and mind, and you can't seem to get enough of it.

You don't "receive love" from somebody else and you don't "give love" to another person—a lover, a father, a mother, a child, a pet, nature, or even our possessions. Love is not a verb, either. It is a feeling, an emotion; it cannot be given or received.

Love is a deeply felt experience you can have when you allow your Self to express through you, when you open the gates of your body and mind and allow the love of your Self to run through you.

From this deep reverence of what loving truly means, it follows that loving yourself entails that you connect with the love that is the essence of your Self and allow that love to run through your entire being. As that happens, you see yourself in terms that are loving, respectful, and kind to the core.

Chances are you have not been taught this way and are not used to the feeling of being so connected to your Self that it pours down your whole body and mind. But it is very important to your healthy state of mind and happiness that you allow yourself to experience the essence of love. This does not come naturally to most people, and so it must be learned.

You have already crossed a few roads since you started this program. You have started to own who you really, really are and are getting in touch with the love that is your Self. Know now that when you're sitting in meditation, love permeates your whole being.

This week's practices will deepen your connection to your Self, and will help you start experiencing self-compassion. They will lead you to practice the feeling of love for the sake of love, instead of as that verb that insists there has to be an external focus of your love.

Just learn and practice how to open yourself to the feeling for now. Later you will find it spreads to everybody in your life.

♋

Self-love, my liege, is not so vile a <u>sin</u>, as self-neglecting.

- William Shakespeare, *Henry V*

Working the Principle

Loving Myself As If I Were My Best Friend

Opening up to love, from easy to hard

This week's practices will train the muscles of love for yourself and others. They will also help you become more aware of beauty and graciousness in the world, and with that awareness you will begin to experience the flow of love from your core to your whole being and then to the outside world.

EXERCISES

1. *Just as I close my eyes at the beginning of my morning and evening meditations I will ask my Self three times:*

> *How does it feel to be Love?*
> *How does it feel to be Love?*
> *How does it feel to be Love?*

Ask from the depth of your heart, with feeling. Do not expect, look for, or speculate on any answer. Just drop the question in the stillness of your Self. Let go of waiting for any answers.

When time is up, stop repeating your mantra or watching your breath and, keeping your eyes closed, say to yourself:

My heart is full of love and compassion.
My heart is full of love and compassion.
My heart is full of love and compassion.

Take a deep breath and open your eyes.

2. I will pay attention to how I feel when I encounter pleasant people and things that I like or appreciate: a puppy, a baby, a sunset, flowers, rain. I will say to myself: I appreciate, like, or love this person, pet, flower, sunset...

Look for reasons and things that you can appreciate today even if they are imaginary. Do not add judgments or reasons for the feeling. Just feel as deeply as you can and stay with the feeling for a few moments.

Try to visualize or imagine that your expression of love for a flower or a sunset is accepted and sent back to you by that flower or that sunset. Truly experience how you feel these emotions in your body and in your mind. Be aware of how love and/or appreciation feel.

Set up sticky-note reminders of this practice around the office, home, car, or purse so you will carry the intention during your active life.

3. I will look at myself in the mirror and will very gently start saying:

I love myself.
I love [state your name].
I love myself.

This can be very difficult at first, but you can do it! The power of this exercise lies in the communication you are initiating with your Self. Start gently: look straight into your eyes. Do not pay attention to the voice of the ego that says, "Who are you kidding?"

It is not about liking your body, hair, etc. This is about you loving all you are, your Self, your divinity, including your body. Do the practice once a day and try to increase the amount of time you spend on it to a minute or more by the end of the week.

Put a sticky-note on your mirror to remind yourself to do it.

4. *I will pay attention to how I react when I or somebody I love makes a mistake. How I deal with it. What kind of help I give.*

Remember how to connect with the pain and suffering by accepting it as a hurt and not as a judgment of failure.

(In addition to your daily meditation, you might want to explore a special kind of meditation that is very nourishing for the soul and deepens your connection with yourself and other people. Visit my website: www.monicabalizan.com– Loving Kindness Meditation.)

FOURTH PRINCIPLE

Thinning the Veil of Judging
Clearing the judging clutter to make room for life

*Out beyond ideas of right-doing and wrong-
doing there is a field. I'll meet you there.*

- Rumi

J udging is our favorite hobby. We are not aware that we have this hobby but we most certainly do.

We spend most of our waking life in critical mode. We judge everything that comes our way. We judge our memories of the past, whatever happens to be going on in the present, and even our expectations for the future. Our constant stream of judgmental commentary is responsible for so much of the noise in our head. It is one of the strongest pollutants of our connection to Self.

Another detrimental effect of this addiction to judging is that our judgment becomes the filter through which we interpret the world. This filter gives us a very partial way of seeing, knowing, and interpreting things, events, people—everything. Our biased views obscure and deform how we relate to life and, as we saw in previous Principles, even to ourselves.

I need to judge because it gives me control! *Really?*

You think that judging helps you organize your world. You get a sense of security and control when you can separate and neatly categorize things and people into the good, the bad, and the ugly. But what you get by doing that is a false sense of security and control, because it is based on your reaction to something and not on the essence of the thing itself, independently of you. When you judge, you form an opinion that is value ridden and that relates much more to you—to all your beliefs, likes, and dislikes—than to the object, the experience, or the person you are judging.

Most of the time we have no idea we are being judgmental. We think we are making observations based on facts, and coming to correct conclusions. Yet much of what you think of as an unbiased opinion is probably a value judgment that clouds your perception of life as it is.

Our habit of judging is one of the things that prevents us from living life from a place of truth. Life becomes a fabrication of our thoughts and judgments that has little relevance to what authentically is in front of us. It is as if we are living life in a separate dimension; instead of living from what is, we are living in the dimension created by our thoughts.

Let's imagine you are walking through a park. Suppose you are aware that you are crossing a park so you notice the sky, trees, flowers, children at play, vendors, smells, noises. Chances are you will start to make critical judgments concerning all the things you notice. The sky may be BEAUTIFUL, but the trees NEED PRUNING, the flowers COULD USE SOME WATER, the PARENTS AREN'T CONTROLLING their children, there are TOO MANY vendors, they should be regulated. Things smell GOOD, things smell BAD, there's TOO MUCH TRAFFIC NOISE.

Without realizing it, you are labeling everything that crosses the radar of your senses. The goods, bads, and all the in-betweens are interfering with your experience of the park as it is, with life unfolding just as it may.

And yes, our incessant judging gives us a sense of control of the world. But of what world? Shakespeare elegantly explains that world when he says in *Hamlet*:

There is nothing wrong or bad, but thinking makes it so.
It delivers to us the world as we wish to see it.

Good or bad, right or wrong?

This model of value judgment that splits the world into good and bad also provides a moralistic framework that, although arbitrary, is heavily weighted to the way we relate to others, ourselves, and life. It is the kind of thinking that underlines most of what we hold to be truth in our societies and in our circles of friends and work. It determines what is good and bad for us. It builds the platform of our beliefs—everything from how to vote to how to pray.

Value loaded judgment is the force behind most fights, wars, acts of terrorism, and any other kind of prejudice that places a divide, that allows us to think we are better than they.

Our Western culture, largely based on the Judeo-Christian tradition, holds quite rigid notions of what is good and bad in our lives. But it does not need to be that way. Eastern cultures, traditionally, keep a more flexible view of what is good and what is bad and of who knows anything with any certainty.

There is a lovely Taoist story that illustrates this point. It goes something like this:

There was an old farmer who had worked his crops for many years. One day his horse ran away. Upon hearing the news, his neighbors came to visit.

"Such bad luck," they said sympathetically.

"Maybe," the farmer replied.

The next morning the horse returned, bringing with it three other wild horses.

"How wonderful," the neighbors exclaimed.

"Maybe," replied the old man.

The following day, his son tried to ride one of the untamed horses, was thrown, and broke his leg. The neighbors again came to offer their sympathy on his misfortune.

"Maybe," answered the farmer.

The day after, military officials came to the village to draft young men into the army. Seeing that the son's leg was broken, they passed him by.

The neighbors congratulated the farmer on how well things had turned out.

"Maybe," said the farmer.

Criticizing others is one of our favorite pastimes. Why do we do it?

Criticism is a form of judgment that is endemic in our culture. It can be a trivial observation about what *she* is wearing, how *he* does his hair, or even how clueless and strange *they* are. It can also be very cruel and damaging to the person or people who are the targets of criticism.

Nowhere is this habit more obvious than in popular culture, where so-called pundits sit in judgment over others in all areas of life—fashion, beauty, talent, morals—and the favorite sport is to eviscerate anyone or anything that is seen as bad, or as not measuring up to the arbitrary standard set by the pundits themselves. This tendency to criticize has led to the billion-dollar industry of reality shows and gossip columns.

It all starts on a much more personal level, however. Often, bonding with others in your group involves talking about non-group members and judging them in ways that lack compassion. This shared critique of someone else cements a bond, affirms a feeling of belonging, of like-mindedness. This habit is deeply ingrained in part because being able to identify with one's "tribe" was once a crucial aspect of remaining safe. It is a survival response that, like so many, is no longer necessary to our survival.

But there is also another reason behind this apparently benign pastime. Criticizing others gives us a sense of superiority. If we criticize someone else's group or "tribe," our own "tribe" becomes stronger in our eyes. And if I criticize another person, I become stronger, it makes me feel more *powerful.* I can plainly see what is wrong in others that they cannot see in themselves. *But is it so?*

When we engage in this kind of judgment, we do so in order to prove ourselves right in an area where we feel or think we're weak. What at some level we believe is wrong or bad in ourselves we see in others. If we didn't have some weakness in the area we are criticizing others for, we would not even notice the issue.

In short, we use the self-righteousness involved in criticism to divert attention from what, at some level, worries us about ourselves.

Suppose you went to the hair salon to have your hair cut and styled and you came out thinking that you looked terrible. Now you have to go out to dinner with office colleagues and you decide you hate your dress, too. At dinner you are feeling insecure or even mortified about the way you look. You cannot enjoy the dinner, you don't even know what you are eating, you're mostly checking how other women look, and they all seem to look better than you. All of a sudden somebody whispers into your ear, "Did you see how much weight Mary put on? What a pity..." This one comment immediately makes you feel better. Somebody else looks worse than you do. You become animated and join in the conversation about Mary's looks. You are safe now. Everybody focuses on Mary and the attention is off you and what you think is your own horrible appearance.

Whenever you catch yourself judging others, stop and remind yourself that perfection does not exist. You aren't perfect and neither is anybody else. Become aware that judging—especially negative, destructive judging—separates you from your Self and restricts you from searching your mind to see what is in you that is making you insecure. Stop to reflect on what is in you that you are projecting onto somebody else with your criticism. Reflect on it and welcome the learning, so you can flourish in creativity and self-love.

Deepak Chopra says that in judging others critically you reflect your lack of self-acceptance, while every person you forgive adds to your self-love.

Can you tame your judging?

It is possible—but it's not easy. As we have seen, we are not used to looking at a person, event, or anything really and just having the experience of that person, event, or thing. Instead, we automatically need to pass judgment—ugly, expensive, pretty, best, hateful—judgments that reflect how we feel or think about the experience and are not inherent to the experience in itself. Even when we understand on an intellectual level that our judgments change with education, age, experience, and other circumstances, we keep judging as if everything is set in stone: we are addicted to it.

Judging is hard to tame not only because it is an acquired habit but because it involves the ego. It is the play of the ego. Remember that ego confuses thoughts, opinions, and judgments with facts. Ego confuses the event with your reaction to that event. *Thus your reaction to a person or an event creates in your mind that person and that event the way you want it to be.* And you stick to your judgment, and you believe it to be so true that you can even fight and go to war to defend it.

The best way I know of judging progressively less is by educating your attention, by training your mind to be vigilant of what it is doing. It requires conscious practice, but as you practice the muscles of your mind into sharper awareness, you'll start to catch your thoughts as they begin to lean towards your usual automatic default judging mode. That noticing will give you the chance to change gears from judging into simply looking at what is now in front of you.

Discernment versus judgment.

When we question our tight relationship with obsessive value judgment, our ego recoils in disgust. It tells us that if we do not assign values to everything we cannot have opinions, and if we don't have opinions we become a total bore, a blimp slouching on a couch nodding.

And yes, you can have opinions and express your likes and dislikes, loves and hates, but they are only interesting when they are born of discernment. Having the ability to discern is what gives you an interesting, wise mind.

Discernment stems from awareness. It is the capacity to see what is actually unfolding in the moment, not judging it but simply noticing it for what it is—independently of you and how you feel.

You may not share somebody's religion but you don't judge him or his religion to be wrong. You may not share someone else's opinion because you have listened and looked at it and you don't agree with it, but you don't judge the other person to be wrong. You choose without judging the other person wrong, better, or worse.

Since it is a quality of awareness, discernment endows your opinions with perceptual clarity and wisdom.

It helps you perceive when your opinion is based on damaging, constricting thoughts and beliefs and when it stems from pure, expansive, and compassionate thoughts, free of limiting beliefs and preconceived ideas. Your opinions endowed with discernment are the kind of opinions that are interesting, evolutionary, and sought after: the kind of opinion that the world needs to heal into peace.

You will always have opinions, so make them count! Base them on discernment, not on value judgment. Slow down your internal judgmental dialogue and open your connection to the discerning wisdom of your Self.

In the previous Principle, we emphasized the psychological and spiritual benefits of practicing self-compassion. We saw that this way of relating to yourself as if you were your best friend can only be practiced by diminishing your negative judgments about yourself. Let's extend now the practice of self-compassion to include compassion towards everybody and everything in our lives, which requires that we suspend our constant value-ridden judgment not only of ourselves but of everything else that crosses our mind's radar. That means you must connect with what is here right now as it presents itself, without the bias of your judgmental commentaries.

You want to get to that place of compassionate living. The closer you get to it, the closer and closer you will get to the incredibly healthy mind that we explored in the First Principle, Awareness. We concluded then that awareness was fundamental to acquiring the beautiful mind that is above all truly happy, and only dwells in compassionate ways—what Matthieu Ricard identifies as the happiest state ever.

♋

Thinking is difficult. That's why most people judge.

- Carl Jung

Working the Principle

Clearing the Judgmental Clutter

Making room for discernment

This week's practices will lead you to begin noticing how much judgment is part of your constant inner voice. They will bring mindfulness to your thought and speech so that you can start to control your automatic judgment. They will prepare you to look at what is in your life without immediate commentary, criticism, or any kind of value judgment. You are working towards exercising discerning opinions rather than value ridden opinions.

EXERCISES

1. *Just as I close my eyes at the beginning of my morning and evening meditations I will drop this intention into the silence of my Self, three times:*

   I will make a conscious choice to notice all the people, things, and events in my day without adding my judgment.

Just sit in the silence of your practice without any expectation, do not dwell in any thoughts or desires for discernment. You are sowing the seed of discernment in the stillness. Know that it will unfold in your Self.

2. I will be very mindful of what I think, do, and feel the moment I meet anybody. If I catch myself ready to judge someone I will stop and do my best to remain neutral toward her. I will give myself the chance to connect to this person as she is in the world without the distortion of my judgment.

Practice using words that describe your feelings and ideas, not universal truths, about people and things. State your preferences, likes, and dislikes, saying "I like it" instead of "this is beautiful," "I think" instead of "it is," "it is convenient for me" instead of "it is convenient for everybody." Exaggerate—you are practicing a new way of seeing the world without your bias.

Remember that what you think, how you see, how you feel about something or someone is "your truth." It is your experience, not necessarily the truth of the experience itself.

3. I will be vigilant in diminishing my tendency to criticize others. When I notice I am judging somebody negatively, I will stop to think what is it in me that I think is wrong and that I am projecting on the other person.

Realize that this is not an exercise to make you feel bad but to make you notice that there is something in you that is bothering you, something you don't like about yourself. Bring it to the light of your Self and find how to work with it in a creative, compassionate way. And that is your way to real *Happiness No Matter What* that flaw might or might not be!

As you exercise this Principle, please make sure that you are very gentle with yourself. You are working at uprooting deeply held beliefs; your ego will not like this new paradigm and will sabotage you as much as possible. Don't give in to the voice that wants to stop you from transforming your life, from one lived in smoke and mirrors to one enriched through the wisdom of your Self.

FIFTH PRINCIPLE

You Are a Powerful Creator!
Own the power of your thoughts and transform your life.

Believe you can and you're halfway there.

- Theodore Roosevelt

This is a tremendously important Principle that posits you as the creator of your life, and it is the Principle that I find the most difficult to talk or write about. I am driven by an urge to make this Principle accessible to as many people as possible, and I need to make it very simple to understand and practice without losing its profound depth. I have striven to convey my best understanding of the theory and the practice so that it is incorporated in your awareness free of magic and with great results.

We are talking about thoughts and how, with them, you create your reality. This is not a new understanding; it has been a basic tenet for thousand of years in all ancient traditions, including the Bible, and today it permeates common wisdom even in the corporate world. *As you think so you are,* says the Bible. More mundanely, Henry Ford said, "If you think you can you can, if you think you cannot you cannot. Either way you are right."

Thousands of pages have been written in the last few decades about the power of thought. They stem from many schools of thought, and most of them have very valid points. I believe that this power is a major asset in our human blueprint, although few people know how to take advantage of it and how to use it to change the course of their lives.

This is not about wishful thinking. I actually find its assumptions annoying and the people who practice it stressed out by so much unmet wishing. In this Principle of creation, we do not negate anything that is happening in ourselves or in our lives. Your clear view and acceptance of the situation you are in is essential, and a basic condition to learning how to work with your thoughts. You aim to see everything as clearly as possible and to acknowledge it. You do not wish the bad away or hide it under the rug away from consciousness. You work with what you have so that you are able to transform it.

What are thoughts made of?

We now know from the findings of quantum physics that everything in the universe is energy. All you see, touch, and sense is made up of corpuscles of energy vibrating at different levels. That includes your body and mine, and the table and the rock in front of me, and it also includes your thoughts and my thoughts.

Einstein elegantly stated it by saying, "What we have called matter is energy whose vibration has been so lowered as to be perceptible to the senses."

We tend to think that our thoughts are sort of "ideas" that happen in our head and don't go anywhere, that they just stay encased inside our skull. But in all reality they are corpuscles of energy fluttering, rippling, and swirling in our minds. And they certainly do not stay there. It is in fact through our thoughts that we interact with the physical universe in a way that what we think affects not only ourselves—our whole body, mind, and soul—but also the world around us.

If you do not think your thoughts are that powerful, just do this little exercise:

> *Close your eyes and imagine that you are having a terrible day, that everybody is against you, that you cannot accomplish anything you set yourself to accomplish. Feel the emotions you are creating, observe how those emotions feel in your heart area. Imagine now that from that constricted state of mind you will interact with people you will be meeting in a few minutes. What do you honestly think will be the quality of the interaction? Not loving and not creative, that is for sure.*

Now close your eyes, and this time:

> *Imagine that you are having a wonderful day, that everybody is supporting you, that you are able to accomplish all you set out to accomplish—and very well. Feel the emotions you are creating, observe how those emotions feel in your heart area. Imagine now that from that expansive state of mind you will interact with people in a few minutes. What do you honestly think will be the quality of the interaction? Not hateful and fearful, that is for sure.*

Can you begin to understand how with your thoughts you create your reality and also influence how the people and even the environment around you feel?

You don't see your thoughts because they carry a much higher vibration than solid objects, like your car or the table, but it does not mean that they are less real than the car or the table. Every time you think a thought, you're sending a specific vibration to the outside world. If it is a positive thought, it has a high frequency. If it is a negative thought, it has a denser, lower frequency.

As we have seen before, the natural state of our Self is one of happiness; as such, it has a very high vibrational frequency. Depending on the quality of your thoughts, you can align with your Self and return to your natural state of being in that high frequency of happiness, or you can hide your connection under the blanket of the slow vibrational frequency of your negative thoughts.

If the only fact we knew about thoughts was that their quality can make us feel good or bad, transforming our lives would be a simple exercise of changing bad for good, unhealthy for healthy, hate for love, poverty for riches. But although that would be a welcome start, it is only the tip of the iceberg. There is so much more behind the simple process of thinking.

In the second Principle, as we unveiled the true nature of who we are, we mentioned the important contribution of quantum physics to that understanding. Max Planck, stating that there is a Matrix where everything originates and everything remains connected to it, gave us a theoretical framework for what all wisdom traditions of the world had known for thousands of years. They did not call it Matrix. They named it the Source, God, the universe, Tao, and so on.

The profound consequence of that "discovery" is that because you are part of the fabric of the Matrix, or Source, you can influence it. You can—and you do all the time. How do you influence the Source of all there is? With your thoughts.

Regardless of the kind of energy your thoughts carry, their vibrational frequencies magnetize corresponding energetic frequencies at the Source, where everything exists. It is a very straightforward process of creation or manifestation, from the thought in your mind to magnetizing similar vibrational energies at the Source, to back to your life and your physical reality.

If, for instance, you think that the world is a dangerous, threatening, unfriendly place, you will always find yourself surrounded by events, people, news, and circumstances that confirm your thought. Everything that supports your worldview will keep coming your way. And this is so because those things you think about and pay attention to, form a collective vibration around you that attracts things and events of the same low vibrational energy of a "terrible world" into your life.

Referring to the energy of love rather than of fear and hate, Marianne Williamson says, "It is an inner way that informs all others." With otherworldly clarity, Einstein is said to have stated, "The most important decision we make is whether we believe we live in a friendly or a hostile universe."

You have created all you have until now.

Maybe you are looking at your life right now and see a few things, or perhaps many things, that you cannot believe, or don't want to accept, that you have created. You probably have done these things unintentionally, because you were not aware of the kind and quality of your thoughts and because you did not know the power of your thoughts. Without that awareness and that knowledge your life has been mostly directed by your unbridled thoughts. You have not taken advantage of the tremendous power of your thoughts to shape your life.

Not owning our thoughts turns us into their puppets and makes our lives quite lusterless.

This is not about blaming yourself or making you feel guilty. On the contrary, this is about empowering yourself to realize the tremendous importance of your thoughts, and as you become more mindful of what you think, what you choose to think, and how you think, you can begin to consciously create the happiness you deserve.

A trained mind prepares you for all aspects of life, good and bad.

Life happens to us, imposing on us events and circumstances that are mostly beyond our control: the sudden death of a perfectly healthy infant, an earthquake that kills our loved ones, children abandoned by their parents. We all know of complicated, sad, and cruel experiences that touch us deeply, and for which we have no apparent answer. I say "apparent," because ancient traditions give answers in terms of previous lives and karmic choices, but that is not the focus of this Principle.

In this Principle, we are working with what we have absolute certainty we can control: our thoughts and how we think. You will learn to see your thoughts and work with them to change your life into a much happier one. And in the process of recreating your own life, you will become much more fitted to deal with those difficult, even excruciating, moments as they show up in your life.

The Process of Consciously Creating

We tend to think that we cannot control our thoughts and that they happen without warning. If we don't train our attention, this is true. We saw in the first Principle that our thoughts, left unchecked, can wreak havoc. But by engaging in this Essential Seven Principles Program, you have been working on training your attention for several weeks now. Your meditation practice from the very first day of this program has slowly but surely been leading you to be more tuned in to your thoughts and what they are doing.

As your meditation practice heightens the clarity and focus of your mind, it is important that you learn how to build on it and consciously create with your thoughts.

Let me introduce you to your powerful Subconscious.

You probably think that your subconscious mind is somewhere in your head, in the back of your brain, and that it is mostly not important. After all, it is "subconscious," meaning not much activity there, a comatose state of consciousness, irrelevant perhaps. But that is wrong, and dangerously so.

You also may think that only the conscious mind is important and it is the centerpiece of your attention. And yes, it is a beautiful and powerful thing to cherish and feed and take care of, but it is not all that is involved in determining how you feel and live. You need to understand the profound role your subconscious mind plays in creating your life.

The subconscious mind works in a very efficient and linear way. When a thought enters your mind and your mind decides it is true or keeps focusing on it, that thought gets imprinted in your subconscious mind. The subconscious mind is completely neutral, it has no opinions, and it just accepts the conscious mind's conclusions and stores them in its files. Although it is neutral and accepting, the subconscious is tremendously effective in vibrating the tune of the thought stored, magnetizing and attracting matching energetic vibrations from the Source.

Let me say this again because it is tremendously important: *Any thought that you repeat over and over in your mind, even if you do it without awareness, becomes a dominant thought. This thought will then be imprinted in your subconscious mind, from which it will vibrate in tune with similar energetic vibrations outside of your mind. It will attract the people, the events, the images, the synchronicities, and everything else that matches that thought.*

Understanding the role of the subconscious highlights once again, the importance of training your mind to pay attention to and observe the quality of your thoughts. And knowing the "rules" of the subconscious allows you to take the steering wheel of your thoughts to create vibrations in your subconscious that correspond to that which you want to manifest.

We have from 60,000 to 80,000 thoughts a day. We saw in our First Principle what our mind left unchecked looks like and how it is congested with irrelevant—if not downright negative—thoughts. Thoughts such as: I can't do it, I'm feeling awful, they'll laugh at me, I'm too old, I'm too young, I don't have experience, I'm not sure, I can't think, I'm overwhelmed, that's out of my league, I don't have enough, I don't have what it takes, I have bad luck, I'm fat, I never, I should, I always, etc., etc., etc...

As you focus on these limiting thoughts, or just mindlessly repeat them, even if you think you are just joking, they are automatically transferred to your subconscious mind. From there, their vibrations magnetize all that is needed to materialize those dysfunctional thoughts into physical realities in your life.

Learning How to Reprogram Your Subconscious

The basic element you will need in order to reprogram your subconscious is—needless to say—your thoughts. Your consciously chosen thoughts are the fundamental units you will use to reprogram your subconscious. With them, you will attract the life that you want.

You have been practicing the Principles of happiness for the last four weeks. Little by little you've been polishing your connection to your Self and Source. You've begun to interrupt the automatic thinking process and become more aware of your thoughts in your formal meditation practice and in your active life. Now you are better positioned to choose your thoughts according to what you want them to bring to you and your life.

These are the few steps that you need to learn and use if you want to reprogram your subconscious:

1. Commit to checking your thoughts as often as possible.

Check to see the kind of thoughts they are, especially if you are not feeling great. Are they blaming, complaining, judging, criticizing, diminishing of ourselves or others? If they are indeed toxic thoughts (or verbal comments), drop them. You don't need them. Change them right away and replace them with ones that are positive or at least neutral. And if you find it's impossible, take a few long and deep breaths and change the whole direction of your thoughts into something completely unrelated for a little while. You can come back to look at them when you are more clear and centered.

2. Carefully choose the thought or thoughts that are associated with what you want to bring into your life.

Try to identify one main thought or combination of thoughts that best describe your dream or desire. See it as clearly as possible.

Start easy: parking space close to the office, getting to the appointment on time. Later on you can work with more transcendental projects. Practice and build your trust one small wish at the time.

3. REPEAT.

The technique that you will use to save those consciously chosen thoughts in your subconscious is REPETITION. Once you choose the thought of what you want in your life and can see it clearly in your mind, repeat that thought again and again.

Repetition helped you learn many things in your life, from the multiplication tables to how to drive a car. Those conscious repetitive learning activities eventually became so automatic that you didn't need to actively think about them again. Repetition "downloaded" the instructions into your subconscious. In this same way you will now download your carefully chosen thought into your subconscious.

You are now entering deeply into the realm of powerful creation.

4. Add feeling and emotion.

Remember that the subconscious is really skilled at vibrating the frequency of a thought once it is stored there. You want to purposely energize that thought to increase its vibrational frequency, and you do that by adding feeling and emotion to your thought. Feeling and emotion charge the energy of your thought. They are the forces that propel your thought into creation.

Visualize and add feeling and emotion to the thought that you want to see manifested in your life, be it a raise, more friends, a life partner, a child—whatever it is. There are no trivial desires; if your desires are good for you, are creative, and contributing to your own and others' happiness, why not wish for them to be fulfilled?

5. *Imagine your dream in the present tense, as if it's already manifested in your life.*

This is a bit more difficult to carry out. But loosen up and practice until you believe it. State your wish in the present tense: *I am enjoying my new fantastic job*, or *I enjoy my fantastic new job*.

Allow yourself to imagine that it's already in your life, that you're already enjoying it, not in the future but right now. Imagine it until you can feel the happiness of the wish fulfilled. Visualize how you want to share it with others. See yourself smiling. You don't know how it happened and you don't care; you just know how crazy fantastic it feels right now. Imagine, visualize, and allow yourself to bask in the glory of your wish already fulfilled.

6. *Release your thought.*

After you have repeated the thought with grand emotion and seen it in your mind already manifested, stop the exercise and let it all go. Just trust and know that your thoughts have created your wish at Source level and that it will come to your physical reality at the right time. You don't know how or when, but don't dwell on that. That kind of thinking will create doubt in your mind. Don't go there. Just know that at the level of Source, it's done.

7. Remain alert to ideas and thoughts that can lead you to take action towards the realization.

It's possible that you'll find yourself being skeptical about this process but let that skepticism go. Suspend your disbelief and give yourself the chance. Just do the practice and you will see how it will work for you.

Neville Goddard, who in his lectures brought forward the concept "Imagination Creates Reality" in a uniquely brilliant and elegant way—and has probably been the most influential teacher on the power of the mind—teaches us to "Assume the feeling of your wish fulfilled and observe the route that your attention follows." And in his book *Your Faith Is Your Fortune* he brilliantly said, "When you drop your desire in consciousness as a seed, confident that it shall appear in its full-blown potential, you have done all that is expected of you. To be worried or concerned about the manner of their unfoldment is to hold these fertile seeds in a mental grasp and, therefore, to prevent them from really maturing to full harvest."

A Word of Caution: Check Your Limiting Beliefs.

Before you attempt to start creating with your thoughts, make sure you know what your beliefs and your belief systems are.

Paying attention to your thoughts and working with them is imperative to steering your life to happier, more peaceful ways, but you also have to pay attention to and examine your belief systems—those stern unquestioned "truths" we live by, and sometimes even die or kill for.

Each one of us has a belief system, a collection of stories we have told ourselves about how things are in the world and of our own truths about how things work or should work. They are sets of statements we firmly believe in and they give us a personal sense of reality and security. The problem is that most of them have been constructed the same way we have created our life, without any conscious, proactive filter.

More often than not, belief systems are built by constricting, debilitating, even stagnating judgments about ourselves, our world, and how things work. They are mainly hand-me-downs from our society, its norms and traditions, and from our own idiosyncratic families. They are "truths" that keep us "safe:" in control and under control. *If you see the hand of the ego behind this construction, you are right.*

Our beliefs are not idle thoughts; they're mostly hard-core prejudices and constricting thoughts that constitute our frame of reference, what we consult to tell us how to live our lives. They are behind the decisions that guide our daily actions.

Our belief systems, when they are based on value judgments (which, as we saw in the previous Principle, do not represent universal truths), do not describe laws of nature, and are not our own discovered truths.

Age, for instance, is a strong and highly constrictive cultural bias, deeply entrenched in our belief system. A three-year-old is supposed to be able to tie his shoes; a fifteen-year-old girl is supposed to start thinking about having a boyfriend; at thirty something you are supposed to be married; at forty a man is supposed to have reached a high point in his career; at fifty men are supposed to be attractive while women are just plain old; at ninety you are supposed to be a vegetable; and so on until you die. Our lives become stratified according to the expectations of "age normalcy" imposed by our belief systems.

Job security is another example of our allegiance to social beliefs, one which sends us on the road of personal stagnation and professional boredom. We stay in jobs that are constrictive, non-inspiring, and overall non-creative because the thought of quitting and looking for something better is deemed "irresponsible." This is a constrictive thought behind a widespread belief system that keeps us safely trapped into lives without luster.

But you can break free from this state of confinement. As you become more vigilant of your thoughts and examine what kinds of beliefs color them, you will want to examine their validity, content, and aim, and separate those born of light and love from those born of darkness, habit and hate.

So, make sure that when you are ready to start creating your dream you examine the beliefs that are behind your dream. Don't allow your unconscious belief system to interfere with the quality or the height and flight of your dream. Allow yourself to dream high, let your imagination soar, allow the glory of your Self to come through. You were born for that.

∽

Sow a thought and reap an act;
Sow an act and reap a habit;
Sow a habit and reap a character;
Sow a character and reap a destiny.

- Ancient Chinese Proverb

Working the Principle

I Create with My Thoughts

I create with the power of my subconscious mind.

This week's practices will lead you to consciously create with your thoughts. They will remind you to be mindful of the quality of your thoughts as well as of your belief systems. They will train you to see if they are life-enhancing and creative or if are they negative and fearful.

EXERCISES

1. *Just as I close my eyes at the beginning of my morning and evening meditations I will ask my Self:*

   "What do I want?"
   "What do I want?"
   "What do I really, really want?"

Dropping this question in the stillness of your Self will start to make you clear on your dreams, what you want to bring into your life that is going to unfold your happiness and peace and that of those around you.

Do not force, expect, or imagine any answers; just know that your Self is listening. You will receive your answers when it is best for you.

2. I will stop to check my thoughts as often as possible during the day.

Are they negative, doubtful, and fearful, or are they happy, healing, loving, and forgiving? If they are not aligned with your Self, stop and change them. If you cannot find anything pleasant to think about a situation, at least remain neutral. Don't allow your thoughts and your beliefs to sabotage your life.

Taking a long and slow breath is a great way to change the state of your mind. Try it!

Set up reminders—maybe a phone alarm to beep once every hour—to remind you to check what kinds of thoughts you are having.

3. I will learn to and practice conscious creation with my thoughts.

Follow the next five steps to becoming a conscious creator of your life in happiness.

☺ **Identify one thing or event what you want to bring into your life.**

START EASY.

You are learning the process of creating with your thoughts, so in the beginning stay with easy, non-emotional wishes. For example: manifesting a dress for the party.

☺ **State your wish in the present tense.**

"I find a great dress for the party."

☺ **Add feeling and emotion.**

Feel as if you are living the wish already come true. Add emotion. Exaggerate.

See it with your imagination, the colors, texture, fragrance, etc. It is not so much about being precise with specific details concerning the manifestation—i.e. the dress—as it is about feeling the emotion that it brings to you as you see it and wear it.

Feel the emotion of wearing that fabulous dress. Imagine the emotion and feelings as you receive compliments. You laugh and swirl around in that beautiful dress… Imagine how happy and loving you feel.

If you experience doubt or feel silly doing this, know that it is the ego talking. Just acknowledge the doubt; treat it as any other negative, diminishing thought. Look at it and then let it go. Don't give in to doubt. Doubting is public enemy number one to your dreams coming true.

☺ **Repeat, Repeat, Repeat**

Repeat your thought or wish in the present tense with as much feeling and emotion as possible until you are comfortable that you have created your desire. You see it in your mind's eye.

It has come true even though you don't see it now in your physical reality.

☺ **Let Go**

Stay attentive to clues that lead you to take appropriate action.

Look for suits in magazines, pay attention to what people are wearing for the particular event you are preparing for, ask questions, be attentive to synchronicities, and so on. Allow yourself to trust the creative process. Don't dwell on the how, just acknowledge your subconscious mind vibrating to the tune of your desire-wish-thought of a beautiful dress.

After you graduate from easy, you can upgrade your desires to more complex creations, such as stimulating and enriching friends, a life partner, a more interesting job, better health, anything you can dream of. Just make it very concrete and clear. Don't be too specific on the details. It's better to dream the general idea. If it's a house, imagine how you feel in each of the rooms, see the light, the warmth, the smells in a wonderful kitchen, etc., but don't add many details, such as the exact shape or number of rooms. You may constrict or limit something that the Universe or Source is bringing to you that is even better and you haven't thought of. Starting easy will help you learn to trust the process.

SIXTH PRINCIPLE

Expressing Your Life Purpose
What's your Dharma?

Let yourself be silently
Drawn by the strange pull
Of what you really love.
It will not lead you astray.

- Rumi

M any of us think or feel that we have a life purpose, and that it is important to find it and align with it. Yet, most of the time we fail badly in our quest to find it and express it. And this is so because we take the wrong road—we take the road of the ego.

Our ego tells us that our purpose has to be something we do or achieve and that it has to be big and important. If I am a doctor, I should be able to find the cure for cancer or at least become very famous; if I am a mother I should write extremely successful books that change the way we bring up children in the world; if I am a teacher, I should be nominated as the most influential teacher on the planet; if I am businessman, I should change the way we do business on the face of the earth. You get the idea.

We associate living our life purpose with something we need to achieve and do so well that others will notice, praise, admire, or even envy us. Living our purpose will make us stand above others. We relate finding our purpose and expressing it to some level of "specialness" that we have or need to have.

Although this belief is common, it's totally wrong, because the premises are all false. It is the ego's interpretation of your life purpose, not your true life purpose. If you follow the path of your ego to find your purpose, you end up frustrated and spiritually empty.

As we stated in Part One of this book, I have a life purpose, you have a life purpose, and everybody else has a life purpose. And it is the same for all of us! Our life purpose is to be happy, to discover happiness and to embody it, to become happiness.

Happiness is your core essence because it is the natural state of your true Self. This program has been bringing you into closer alignment with your Self. Gradually you are beginning to percolate some of the attributes of your Self into your daily life. As you realize that, you will indeed agree that it is a real triumph in itself! You have been adding a drop of happiness and peace into your life day after day. Regardless of what your ego might be telling you, by working with this program you're on the right path to living your purpose.

This is a great start to enjoying a wonderful life. *But you have to remember that your purpose is to be happy not just for yourself or your self-realization or because it's pleasant to be happy.* You are not alone in this planet—everything you do, every step you take, impacts those around you and beyond. Your life purpose is enmeshed with everybody else's in this world. Your gradual transformation into who you really are has ripple effects on the whole planet, on everybody and everything in it, making it a kinder, more peaceful place to live.

As you can see, this deep and true meaning of your life purpose has nothing to do with the grandiose ideas your ego whispers to you and that you, in a moment of weakness or forgetfulness, believe. The question is, how can you express your purpose? How can you contribute to enhancing the beauty of this world? Where do you get what you need to put your purpose to the service of the world? It really sounds like a daunting—or at least a tremendously difficult—task!

Your Gifts and Your Talents

Indeed, we all came to this world to *become* happiness. *How we express our purpose is unique to each one of us.* It is a reflection of the gifts and talents that each one of us has. Yes, you have been born with your own individual gifts and talents, and as you discover and express them in your daily life you'll be happier, more fulfilled.

Your gifts are threaded through your soul, that is why when you use them, you align with the peace of your Self. Conversely, when you don't use or develop them, you feel there's something missing in your life and have a longing that you cannot intellectually express.

Deepak Chopra explains that longing beautifully as the call of the soul for you to give expression to the gods and goddesses you brought with you to this world and that are still in your soul, waiting for you to unfold and cultivate them *in service to humanity.* When you heed the call of your Self to live your purpose, your life makes sense and you are at peace with it. This is Chopra's poetic and succinct take on the law of Dharma, a concept very developed and important in the Vedic tradition, that goes even further to say that when you unfold and develop those unique talents, they find their match in unique needs out in the world.

It's quite a tall order to explore and develop your talents so as to express them by fulfilling specific needs in the world! But once you understand that the manifestation of your purpose is supported by your innate skills and gifts, finding out what they are becomes a joyful and creative process.

We have all had glimpses of a special kind of joy, those enriching moments when you realize that something you say or do is meeting someone else's needs, that you're contributing in some way to a person's happiness, relief, or peace. The nature of the interaction doesn't matter, nor does it matter how large or small you think that exchange is. What's important here is the realization of the gift that that "small" expression of your talents brings to another person—and also to yourself. You feel great, even if only for a moment, and it's because your action is aligned with your life purpose manifesting itself through one of your unique talents. *That joy you feel in those moments is the tingling sensation of your life purpose being expressed through a skill that makes somebody else's life a bit better.*

This Principle will help you discover and know which are your particular talents so that you can creatively and consciously express them. And as you do, they will start to meet the need for them in the external world. Following your Dharma, you will find yourself more and more joyful and successful.

Most of us think that our talents are directly related to our jobs, or to what we do for living. Sometimes they are, but most often not.

One of my clients, a sought-after financial planner, came to see me because although her business was booming, she could not find happiness in it. She felt something was missing. We worked for a while on finding her special talents, and at one point she realized she'd always been very good at remodeling and decorating homes, that she'd helped all her friends and family when they needed help, and that her contribution had helped them sell their houses at a much higher price. She logically concluded that one of her unique gifts had to be decorating, and was considering giving up her financial planning practice to start a remodeling career. She'd reached a tempting conclusion, but after spending some more time with the exercises in the Essential Seven Principles Program, she realized that yes, she enjoyed remodeling and it came easily to her, but what really motivated her was helping others, seeing how her help made them happier, and because of that she was also contributing to her own happiness.

Helping others was one of her special gifts. Decorating was one of the channels that she could use to express her gift of compassion, but not the only one. She could use her talent to help people in whatever situation they showed up in her life. She further realized that if she chose to stay in her financial office, she'd become more aware of how much she and her advice could help her clients. Looking for ways to deliver compassion by helping clients deeply connected her to her life purpose.

How do you identify your skills and talents?

Ask your Self to help you discover those skills and talents that give your life meaning and purpose. Your Self knows you.

As you are getting more familiar with your Self through your daily meditation, ask your Self to help you. Pose the question to your Self and stay open. Just trust that you will have the answer when you are ready

Make a list of all the things that you like to do so much that while you are doing them, you are happy, you are passionate, and you don't mind the passing of time—in fact, you lose all sense of time. Do not limit yourself to what makes sense. The items in your list can include anything—gardening, running, studying, public speaking, meditating, visiting friends, traveling, being a mother, being a surgeon, being a carpenter, recycling. Do not limit yourself to things you enjoy in the present, but include past activities and moments that felt especially joyful and fulfilling. Go as far back into the past as you like.

Study your list for clues that indicate a constant in your life. Look to identify the things that you have always enjoyed, even if they have changed in form or shape as you grew older. For example, listening to other people's stories or problems. That theme or constant throughout your life may be a clue that leads you to identify your talent in understanding and listening to people; maybe you want it to unfold in a job such as social work or teaching, or perhaps you want to hone it to consciously use it as a mother, or while interacting with friends or colleagues, or with people in general. What a gift to give to your people and to the world!

Becoming aware of your skills is very important. It guides you into doing whatever you do in life with a newer perspective and a clearer awareness of why you are doing it, or how to better do it, so that it expresses your uniqueness in a more fulfilling way.

As you are working at identifying your talents, pay attention to what shows up in your life and those situations that bring a spark of happiness to you. See them as hints from your Self about your gifts supporting your life purpose.

You will know you are living your life purpose when your life becomes joyfully exciting.

Check that your *intentions* match your life purpose.

Your intentions can lead you to the joyful accomplishment of your life purpose or derail you from it. Becoming aware of what your intentions are at any given moment will allow you to choose the road of happiness and success.

Intention is not a thought. It is much more than a thought. Intention is the overarching force behind everything that exists and everything you do or don't do.

Everything that we know starts as an intention and comes to life by the power of that intention. Every one of your decisions, big or small, that leads to getting, achieving, reaching, feeling, conquering something in your life, is fueled by the underlying force of your intention. Your intentions are behind everything you choose every day of your life. It's a tremendous force that, when you know how to use it, makes your life much more enjoyable.

As you become aware of the power of your intentions you will want to identify them so you can make sure that they are on track with your life purpose, and that they are not taking you the wrong way.

Intentions are to your gifts and life purpose what stop signs and detour flags are to a destination map. You need to learn to check on them, otherwise you might fall into the ocean while aiming for the Sahara Desert.

Intentions are not static, set in stone. They change all the time according to where you are in your life at a given moment. Suppose that you just had your first baby, and one of your conscious intentions is to become a healthier woman, to achieve the energetic, healthy, and strong body necessary in order to bring up your baby. That is your intention for this moment in your life, and it's in alignment with your life purpose of embodying happiness, expressed as being a loving, dependable, giving mother. Being the best mother you can be, and knowing that you are, fills you with joy and purpose.

So you're aware of this intention and you set up specific steps to get to that healthy body you want to achieve. You establish a daily routine of physical activity, going to the gym, running, whatever it is, and you also decide on what you're going to feed yourself, how you're going to hydrate your body, and so on. The specific action steps you take are closely aligned with your Self and largely with your primordial intention. That alignment to Self and Source will provide the force of your intention that will support your decision.

Understanding the intentions that underlie your decisions is crucial to keeping you in sync with your life purpose.

Being aware of what your intention is when you are doing what you are doing and deciding what you are deciding is a powerful way to steer the direction of your life towards happiness. If you are like most of us, you don't know what your intention is behind much of what you do. You simply make decisions based on the past, your experience, what feels right this moment, or—even worse—without reflecting on what is best at all.

But if you want to align with your life purpose, you will want to make sure your intentions are truly in harmony with it. If you are not sure at any given moment what your intention is for making a certain decision, stop and ask your Self. Once again, your Self is your best ally, your Self knows what your intentions are and how well they match your purpose.

Say that you are pretty certain that Rob will propose marriage to you and you don't know how to respond. It is a big decision and a big step in your life. But you are just not sure or comfortable with either yes or no as an answer. You are doubly surprised at your doubt because you have been dreaming of this moment, and yet... you are not sure and you don't know what to do. If you remember that your Self is your best friend, you would ask your Self what to do. You would make your Self your accomplice in realizing your life purpose.

"Is my decision to marry Rob aligned with my life purpose?"

"Will my skills and talents be of service and joy to this marriage?"

"What is the intention behind my acceptance or denial of the proposed marriage?"

Know that you will receive the answers.

Your body can also tell you a lot about your mind. When you pose the questions to your Self, pay attention to how you feel when you're asking them. Is your body relaxed, energized, open, and free, or do you feel you're constricted, tight, and fearful all over? Your body can give you great information: pay attention to it.

This is an example concerning a marriage decision, but it can be applied to anything that you're thinking, deciding, or doing. It can be a question of your intention to move to a new country, join Doctors Without Borders, buy a particular house, or even whether to eat another piece of cake or not.

It is very helpful—even necessary—to get in the habit of checking on your intentions and asking your Self when you're not sure if they are in your highest interest. Stay flexible and don't just deny the nagging whispers that invite you to change course or to start something completely new. Don't negate your insights. If you're not totally sure, go back to asking your Self, but remain open to what shows up.

Everything in the universe is in constant movement. Life is fluid. But you need to know that when you start working with your life purpose, you evolve and expand at an even faster pace. So expect change and accept that nothing is rigid or set in stone. Welcome change!

You are now shifting your life so that it is aligned with your life purpose. Your life purpose will be the rising star at the end of the road, beckoning you to follow its light. As you travel you'll meet flags and icons telling you at each point where you are and what your options are, to use your skills, to stop, to rest, to continue, to recharge, to change the route. These flags provide you with opportunities to strengthen your awareness of what your intentions are and how to use your skills and talents so that you can decide with clarity of purpose. They give you a chance to steer the wheel back toward the star. Your focused intention will provide a smooth and successful trip.

Intentions? Why not goals?

There is a frenzy and a hype about having goals. There are classes, seminars, and books of all kinds teaching the importance of goals and how to set them up for success. We're convinced of the need to have them. We hope that if we accomplish our goals, we will finally become rich, healthy, glamorous, successful, peaceful, or maybe even happy.

We choose our birthday, first day of work, first day of vacation, wedding anniversary, or other iconic days to start working toward our goals. The favorite day of the year for this goal-setting is New Year's Day. We have all been there. We've resolved to quit smoking, lose weight, go to the gym, sleep eight hours a day, spend more time with the family, get a new job, finally have the talk with the boss, drink more water, be more positive, more forgiving, and so on. These are wonderfully virtuous declarations of specific goals that by the end of January are mostly forgotten, and when remembered they only bring us frustration and guilt.

Goals, as they are commonly understood, are specific outcomes that we want to achieve. They always seem like good ideas. But then why is their success rate so low? Why is the practice of setting up and reaching goals mostly inefficient, and if we are successful, why is it only after a lot of work and sacrifice?

It is so because your goals are not usually aligned with your true nature, your Self, but with your intellect. They rely and depend solely on your sheer willpower to achieve. There is no unfolding of your natural skills, no joyful results for you and those close to you.

Another deterrent to the fulfillment of goals set up by the intellect alone is that they are mostly ego-induced, and so they are shaded with fear. You want to lose weight to look better than your friends or so that your partner will not leave you; you want to keep the relationship so that you don't loose your status; and so on. This ego-based fear at the foundation of your goals will direct the force of the intention toward the fear that is motivating them and away from the change your intellect is hoping for. And that is why you have to work so hard at reaching your goals.

Mallika Chopra says it best when she says that intentions come from the soul, while goals come from the mind. Goals do not have the divine force of the Self to propel you into what you want to create.

The practices that follow will help you become aware of your intentions and see how they can best serve your life purpose. Train yourself to align them with Self and witness your life become much more effortlessly happier.

༄

Seek out that particular mental attribute which makes you feel most deeply and vitally alive, along with which comes the inner voice which says, "This is the real me," and when you have found that attitude, follow it.

- William James, *Principles of Psychology*

Working the Principle

My life purpose is supported by my intentions!

I am discovering my gifts and talents.

This week's practices will lead you to begin discovering your unique gifts so that you can express them in alignment with your life purpose. You will also strengthen your awareness of what your intentions are and how they harmonize with your life purpose.

EXERCISES

1. *Just as I close my eyes at the beginning of my morning and evening meditations I will ask my Self three times:*

   "What is my dharma?"
   "What are my talents and gifts?"
   "How can I use them to serve others?"

Once again, do not expect, speculate, or think about any answers. Just ask and trust the process. Be vigilant for signs and coincidences that will show up in your daily life. They are clues to the answers to your questions.

2. *I will start to discover my gifts and talents.*

Find a quiet place to make a list of your innate gifts.

Get paper and pen—you will be writing for a while.

Set the alarm to ring in 15 minutes.

Now ask yourself the questions:

☺ *"If time and money were not an issue, what would I do that would bring me happiness?"*

☺ *"What is it that I like so much that when I do it I am happy and lose all sense of time?"*

Don't think about your answers. Just write whatever comes to your mind. Try to not lift the pen, and do not edit your writing. Just write. If after the first 5 minutes you run out of ideas, start again, and keep going for the remainder of the 15 minutes. Just keep on writing. There is no right or wrong answer.

When time is up, stop writing.

Study your list and see if there is a thread that ties some things, interests, activities, wishes together. That thread is most likely a clue to your most striking gift or gifts.

Keep asking the questions and writing your answers every day until you feel comfortable with the leads you find in your answers. Start thinking about how you would like to express them now.

Stay alert for what shows up.

3. *I will be mindful of the intentions behind my choices and decisions.*

As decisions and choices come up during the day I will ask myself:
"What is my intention behind this decision?"

"Is it aligned with my life purpose? Is this my best choice?"

Once again this exercise asks you to be as aware as possible of how you feel about a particular intention behind your decision. Try to notice how it feels. Is it heart-opening and loving, or does it feel tight and take you away from your connection to your Self? Stay flexible and open to new ideas as well as to old ones. Just look at them, and if they appeal to you explore them and see where they lead you. You are now skillful in knowing where they are coming from: ego or Self?

SEVENTH PRINCIPLE

Gratitude: The Crown Jewel of Transformation
Gratitude is the secret key to Grace.

If the only prayer you will say in your entire
life is "thank you" that will be enough.

- Meister Eckhart, German Theologian

W e have arrived at the seventh and final Principle. My favorite Principle. It is so much so that I can truthfully say that if for any reason you remember only one of the Principles, this is the one to stick to and never leave behind.

The practice of the previous six Principles has incrementally polished your connection to Self, and now you are in a great, receptive place to fully appreciate and incorporate the full reach and richness of the practice of gratitude.

Gratitude is a very powerful force that transforms your life in all ways. The energy of gratitude is unique. It opens up your connection to Self and lights up the path for grace to flow. Gratitude allows you to dwell in a state of consciousness known as the state of grace.

What is *Grace?*

In everyday life we use the word grace to describe a person's finesse or charismatic bearing, or to refer to a dignified favor we receive or give, as when we forgive or are forgiven.

But grace is most commonly related to religion. In Western religions, grace is a form of blessing bestowed from a god to his people. In Eastern religions, although called by different names, it denotes a highly appreciated gift passed from a guru or teacher to her followers. In all cases grace refers to something very special that is given to us by god or a teacher. It's a special gift that comes *from outside* of us.

In this Principle I do not use the term in its religious context, although Pope Frances recently described grace as the "amount of light in our souls." And yes, grace is the light in your soul. It isn't outside of you. No exterior power or person bestows it upon you. Grace is the state of your true Self.

Grace is an attribute of your true Self that you either let shine or dim, but it is part of who you are and it is always with you. *The Vedic tradition elegantly refers to grace as god within.*

We all feel the light of grace at some point in our lives. You've probably not recognized it or named it grace, but I'm sure you can think of a few instances of utter joy and contentment. And that is the experience of grace bathing every cell of your body and corner of your mind.

The experience of grace is unique to each one of us, but you'll know grace is active in you when you feel the special warmth of beauty and wellness in your heart rippling through your whole body and mind. Grace is joy, and it's the essence of those moments. Grace is what you sometimes express with a heartfelt "thank god!" and "I'm so happy!"

You can feel grace distinctly when you are fully present, immersed in nature, tuned in to the softness of the dew in the woods, or absorbing the hypnotic depth of a sunset at the beach. Your whole being feels the experience as a soft landing on the essence of perfection. Even if it's only a moment.

Grace is an incredibly joyful state of mind that's so complete that when you recognize it you want to keep it forever, and you also want to give it to everybody else in the world! *What a heaven on earth you'll start!*

We are not there yet, but with practice we can begin to consciously make grace ours. The effects of your living a life more and more inspired by grace will ripple out into your world in no time.

How do you attain grace? The best way I know of is by activating your connection to your Self through gratitude. Deepak Chopra calls gratitude the secret key to grace.

What is *Gratitude*?

Gratitude is not a passing thought or a word of thankfulness. It is not that automatic polite thank you of quick acknowledgment when somebody opens the door for us or tells us the time. Those are nice habits of good manners and polite behavior, but usually performed without depth of feeling, and they're short lived.

Gratitude is the golden key that miraculously opens the gates of your real Self and floods your whole being with joy and truth. It is the immediate path to grace.

Gratitude is a distinct state of deep appreciation, of awareness of the bountiful ways of the cosmos and of the gifts that the universe provides to you. You can only be in this state of appreciation when you're present and fully connected to the experience of the moment, so you are truly able to notice and see what there is to be grateful for. If you're not present, you miss the opportunity to feel gratitude and for gratitude to work its magic.

The next key requirement for establishing gratitude in your awareness is the "good health" of your perceptions. The way you perceive and interpret the world affects your ability to be grateful. If your perception of the world is clouded and blocked by negativity, limiting beliefs, resistance to what is, and control issues, your path to grace is severely limited.

A True Anecdote

> *Two friends go on a trip to a small island. When they arrive at their destination, it starts to rain. Mark becomes angry, sighs loudly, shakes his head in frustration, tightens his fists, and, throwing up his arms in defeat, explodes: "it had to happen, it always happens to me, wherever I go it rains and I have a miserable time, I have such bad luck, it's the only time of the year I can get a vacation and it rains. I wish I was back home. Whole trip is spoiled now!"*
>
> *To which Chad calmly replies, "I think it's great that it's raining! It'll give us an excuse to rest and relax before dinner, instead of rushing to check out the beach and the area. We'll stay in town, have dinner at a local restaurant, and maybe we can meet the natives who can tell us all about the hidden treasures on the island."*

Two different perceptions of the same rainy experience. Which perception is life-enhancing? Who do you think will end up having a peaceful and happy experience? As long as Mark keeps his perception of the situation unchanged, he'll remain closed and blocked to any hint of gratitude. Just as he thought, he will probably end up having a very annoying time. Chad's perception is instead open to appreciating everything that shows up, and finding the hidden treasure every step of the trip. Chad will most surely have a great vacation, in spite of his travelling companion.

A Course in Miracles says that a miracle is a shift in perception. It also says that the angels are thoughts of god sent to us as messengers of love—or perceptions of love. I don't think this refers to negative, judgmental perceptions but to evolutionary, healing ones.

We learned in the Fifth Principle that if your thoughts are shaped by fear and mistrust, negativity is the source of your perceptions. The negative quality of your perceptions, without a doubt, blocks you from experiencing the peace of gratitude.

You owe it to yourself to take inventory of your thoughts. What are your thoughts about life in general, people, your friends, your work, your family? Examine them objectively and remove all dark ones from the repertoire you hold in your mind. Take a scalpel to your mind and excise all the negative, pessimistic, fearful thoughts and replace them with positive, kind, creative, and life-enhancing ones. Or, if you cannot do so right now, at least replace them with neutral ones. One thought at a time.

If you think that once you start removing your negative beliefs, your "heart-held core truths," you will lose your edge, take a look at what Wallace Wattles, a highly influential thinker and the author of *The Science of Getting Rich*, said: "You cannot exercise much power without gratitude, because it's gratitude that keeps you connected to power."

Here's to Gratitude!

The new neuroscience of epigenetics shows that what you think as well as what you do affects every single cell in your body, including your gene activity. Your positive, appreciative thoughts and ways of looking at life can even generate new brain cells and new pathways identified with happiness.

As you engage in expressing gratitude, you can shift stress and depression into psychological states such as compassion and empathy. Deepak Chopra and Rudolph Tanzi, in their book *Super Genes,* say that positive, loving thoughts can shift your genetic activity in a positive wellness direction that includes a stronger immune system, more energy, ridding yourself of persistent aches and pains, normalizing metabolism, decreasing the risk of cancer, and even slowing the aging process.

In a word, gratitude connects you with your deepest Self, and you feel that connection as peace and light while at the same time benefitting your entire physiological body.

Feeling Gratitude Even When Life Gets Tough

Most people choose to be thankful for good health, good relationships, good income, good homes, etc. I haven't yet met anybody who is grateful for "bad" things, such as illness, violence, death, theft, corruption, or treason. I believe our minds aren't wired to be thankful for negativity in our lives. Trying to be thankful for negativity would mean denying a stark reality that is hurting us, and would be detrimental to a healthy state of mind. Besides, how can we find the light in the darkness if we deny there is darkness to begin with?

Negativity in all its aspects abounds, and you should neither deny it nor succumb to it. Instead, you can learn to appreciate the glory of life with all its imperfections. This doesn't mean that you resign yourself to pain and hurt and prefer it to happiness. It does mean that you're also aware that every day has moments of beauty, love, generosity, appreciation, kindness, altruism, truth, sweetness, and compassion.

Let's look again at the passage in Hermann Hesse's *Siddhartha*, which we referred to in Part One of this book, as Siddhartha understood the essential nature of life and how even in the midst of chaos he could still find his intrinsic joy. That knowledge and awareness that chaos is part of life, and that even in the midst of the hurt and sorrow you can find ways to experience gratitude, will lead you to start shedding light into the darkness of your sorrow.

When you become established in gratitude and appreciation, you drop the drama and the victimization every time you get bad news or confront obstacles. Gratitude takes you into the ways of peace, where you can see the obstacles and even the tragedy with deep trust and knowingness.

I had the privilege to witness from one of my clients the most striking example of how gratitude can find its way even in the darkest hours of the human experience. She had been my client for a few years and was now coming to see me only sporadically for "touch ups." She was a young, bright, hard-working corporate lawyer, the single mother of a ten-year-old son. Her professional career was extremely demanding and she had to work on not feeling guilty because she could not spend enough time with her son. Her young son was the true love and light of her life.

One morning the phone rang. It was Catherine hysterically crying, asking me to please see her the next day. In a burst of desperation she explained that her son had just been diagnosed with terminal cancer, and that he had three months to live. I was in such deep sorrow and shock, I cancelled all appointments for the rest of the day, thinking, contemplating, and asking Self for the wisdom that would allow me to help her. But I could not find anything that I could say or do that I felt would help her in a transcendental way.

When morning came, I still had no idea of how and if I would be able to help at all. She was living the worst suffering I believe a human being can bear in life. When she finally arrived, we hugged and sat on the sofa and she kept crying for a long time without speaking. After a while, I could sense that something was starting to happen, something was shifting in her. Eventually she became very silent and very peaceful and all of a sudden she said to me, "I am so incredibly grateful and thankful that I am here to take care of my son in his last months. My love for him will transform this experience so much. I cannot imagine what would have happened to him if I wasn't here and he was alone living this terrible illness. I'm here for him!"

My client's gratitude took her to the light of grace that dispersed the shadows of her horrific pain and she was able to be a peaceful, loving presence to her son until the very end.

Gratitude is not easy to bring to mind when the going gets tough. This is an undeniable truth. Life is not a bed of roses, and if it is, the thorns are never far away. We prefer the roses to the thorns, but don't deny anything that comes our way. Instead, look everything in the face and accept it. When pain and sickness come into our life, we know how to cry and be sad, but also know that it's possible to bring love and light into the experience, that we can connect with Self. Gratitude is the easiest path into the light of Self.

If you are prepared, you'll be ready to embrace gratitude.

If you're not prepared, if gratitude is not a constant in your life, you will most likely forget about finding a reason to be grateful when things don't happen as you expected, or when they're abysmally different. You won't even want to hear about grace. You'll probably get into a rage and bang walls and scream, blame and judge people, god, and yourself. If unprepared, you'll disconnect from Self and grace and this will lead you to become a total wreck, left alone with your ego.

The way to make sure that you can find the path to gratitude and to the wisdom of the Self in those testing moments in your life is by being prepared for them. You prepare by strengthening your awareness of gratitude, which means that you have to practice it again and again. You train yourself to be in the state of gratitude until it's ingrained in your body and mind.

In the same way that you practice running a marathon for months, if not years, before the actual date, you practice gratitude before the ball drops. It is possible but not easily done.

Train yourself into gratitude until it's a habit you cannot kick.

Some people find it difficult in the beginning to express gratitude. If you feel that way too, it is ok. Don't force your feelings. If you don't feel gratitude start with a sense of general "appreciation."

Appreciate the weather, the smell of baked bread, maybe your children if they're having a good day, a pet, a sunset, a tree on your block, even your eyes or your hair. Think of all the people who have helped you in your life and those that today help you, even people you don't know but are essential for you to have what you have now, from the bus driver or doorman to the farmer in the fields. They are all participants in the Universe helping you to live your life. Be thankful for that. And if all else fails, be thankful that you can read—there are millions of people who can't. Anything to start you getting acquainted with the feeling of appreciation. Notice how it's warming up your body and how good it feels.

If all fails, fake the feeling of appreciation. In time gratitude will penetrate your mind and body and you will become gratitude.

Gratitude for what you have, for what the universe is bestowing upon you, for the perfection of what is here now, does not mean that you don't want to improve or enrich many areas in your life. What it means is that while you appreciate what you have now for many reasons, you also wish for and work to have a more rewarding job, recognition, inspiring friends, new relationship, children, a better car, or perfect health. Being truly grateful has nothing to do with being passive, without ambitions and desires.

Once you understand the deep benefits that living in the state of grace that gratitude brings to your body, mind, and spirit, the task of walking the path of gratitude is not very difficult. It will actually enrich your life in happy, peaceful ways.

♋

At times, our own light goes out and is rekindled by a spark from another person. Each of us has cause to think with deep gratitude of those who have lighted the flame within us.

- Albert Schweitzer

Gratitude opens the door to the power, the wisdom, the creativity of the Universe.

- Deepak Chopra

Working the Principle

I Am Grateful!

Opening the channels to the peace and happiness of grace

This week's practices will begin to establish gratitude as the default state in which to live your life. They will strengthen your ability to be present, to connect to what is happening in the moment so as to notice things, events, and people to be grateful for. They will also deepen your awareness of the quality of your perception, so that when it moves into denying the grace of gratitude, you can move it back in alignment with the true nature of your Self.

EXERCISES

1. *Just as I close my eyes at the beginning of my morning and evening meditations I will ask my self:*

> *"What am I grateful for?"*
> *"What am I grateful for?"*
> *"What am I grateful for?"*

Don't seek or expect answers while you you're meditating. Just drop the seeds in the silence of your Self.

During your active day look for and pay attention to reasons to be grateful.

2. Today and every day I will find at least five reasons to be grateful. I will say "thank you" to each one of those reasons and will stay with the feeling of gratitude as long as possible.

Start out with the easy things: your pets, a friend, your eyes that let you read, your ability to walk—even gratitude for your breath that keeps you alive. After a while you can move your gratitude to other things and people, and it will be easier and very rewarding.

Take a walk in nature, even if it's just a park or a backyard, and allow yourself to feel appreciation for nature's generous beauty. Even observing the perfect harmony of a tree will serve you. If you cannot go outside, go on the internet and check out the wonders of the world; stay in awe and appreciation.

Spend some time experiencing the <u>feeling</u> of gratitude. If you cannot feel it, think it or imagine it: exaggerate it. Have fun with gratitude! That will start to loosen your gratitude muscles. Stay with the experience even if for just a moment.

3. I'll make a list of the people who have taught me something, who are or have been my friends, and who have helped me in any way. I will write thank you notes. Even if I don't actually send them. I will open my heart to these people in gratitude for being in my life in their own unique way.

I will keep the list handy so I can add names to it.

The more people you can say thank you to, the better. Don't limit the list to your friends; include the person who opened the door for you at the store, the cashier at the supermarket, the waiter at the restaurant, everybody that shows up in your life and is doing their best to serve you. Don't just say "thank you," try to add feeling to it. Look for occasions to say thank you even if only mentally.

4. *I will set a timer to buzz me at least three times a day. It will remind me to check on my perceptions of gratitude. I will ask myself:*

   "What are the thoughts animating what I'm doing?"
   If they aren't aligned with gratitude, I'll change them.
   I will ask grace to help me stay the course in gratitude.

Experience the feeling of gratitude and aim for more and more. Little by little you'll become gratitude, and you'll dwell in a state of grace in all its light and ***Happiness No Matter What!***

PART THREE

THE END—WHERE IT ALL BEGINS

What we call the beginning is often the end. And to make an end is to make a beginning. The end is where we start from.

- T. S. Eliot

Now this is not the end. It is not even the beginning of the end. But it is, perhaps, the end of the beginning.

- Winston Churchill

We have travelled together for seven weeks, one Principle a week. It is time now for you to begin exploring your new life armed with new awareness, skills, and powerful tools. You are now empowered to begin a life of happiness and success *No Matter What.*

You have opened the coffers containing the treasures of your true nature. You've looked at them and rescued them from the debris of clueless conditioning and dull awareness. You're now established in the truth of your Self and you're ready to keep its beauty alive and its light flowing through all of you and those whose lives you touch.

The Program has unveiled your hidden and forgotten powers, and you have started to use them consciously to illumine your life and help lighten the shadows of those around you. As you opened up to the premise that your true essence, your Self, has infinite potential, is perfect in every way, and is imbued with creativity, peace, and happiness, you began to allow those attributes to permeate your mind, body, and life.

The practices you have been exercising are establishing habits in your thinking, perception, and ways of behaving that keep the connection to your true essence polished and pliable.

As you continue training throughout your life, that connection to your Self will become the backbone of your daily life. It will be ready and available for you when life is easy, and especially when it is not so easy—those moments when you need to touch and feel even more peace and light.

Life is a wonderful and miraculous experience, and by working with this Seven Principles Program you have begun to claim your power over how you live it. It's up to you how you choose to surf the waves of life, the ups and downs and the in-betweens. And just as we practice surfing in the water so we're ready when the big wave shows up, we practice being from our true Self, deeply connected to it, so that when the big wave of life hits the shore, we're ready.

You're preparing yourself to catch opportunities for beauty and love of all kinds, and also to be unbreakable when you're forced to live sad, scary, and lonely moments. You'll cry and be heartbroken but you'll not resist the moment; you'll look at your experience as it unfolds with a "knowing," a sacred "spaciousness," that will shed light into your sorrow and love into your entire being.

As I promised in the beginning, I promise now in the end: If you commit to a few minutes a day to expand and deepen your meditation practice and continue to do your habit-forming exercises, your life will deeply transform, and one day you'll realize that you are living Happiness No Matter What.

The roadmap has been drawn and it's yours. As you tread it with commitment, patience, and trust, you leave your footprints on fertile soil, and they'll remain there to show you the way back home when you become forgetful.

As you start on your travels empowered by new habits and a heart full of peace, don't compromise your Self, but know that the road is not a straight, predictable one from beginning to end. Together with the beautiful views and side scenery there are bumps and hills and unexpected turns. You are equipped to face them and navigate them but the most dangerous one you'll ever encounter will be the one that happens when you are not present, when your awareness is somehow foggy. When that happens, as you realize your mind is absent, I hope you will be generous enough to forgive yourself. Better yet, pat yourself on the back for having noticed, and go back to aligning with the magnificent Self you are.

You can do it; this Seven Principles Program has given you the tools you need to go back to alignment with your Self. Keep practicing them after the seven weeks are finished. Review them every now and then and reflect on how else you can include them in your daily life.

Now that you're aware of all you are and can bring into your life and the life of those around you and beyond, commit to live from it and don't negotiate your integrity, your truth.

Polish your focus and awareness to choose your life as only you from Self can do it, from love and happiness. Treat yourself to it!

I cheer for your voyage into *Happiness No Matter What!*

With immense gratitude,
Monica

APPENDIX

Mantra Meditation

Some people find it easier to meditate by focusing their attention on a mantra rather than on the breath. Mantra is a Sanskrit word that means vehicle, it can be a single word or group of words that are used to help quiet the mind. Instead of the breath, you focus your attention on the mantra. We use mantras mostly in Sanskrit, but they can be words in any language.

For our purpose of quieting the mind and training our attention, I prefer mantras/words that do not have any strong connotations or emotions associated with them. Unless it is a mantra specifically appointed to you according to certain facts of your birth as in Primordial Sound Meditation or a mantra chosen for a particularly energetic vibration, I like to teach the mantra "so hum." It reflects the sound of the breath and roughly means "I am."

Mantra Meditation Instructions

1. Choose a place as quiet as possible and where you will not be disturbed. Preferably, dim the lights a bit, just gentle reading light, but avoid total darkness.

2. Silence your phone. I recommend airplane mode with the wireless off (so texts don't come through), so you can still use your timer. Set the timer for 10 or 15 minutes, ideally 20.

3. Sit comfortably, on a chair or on a cushion on the floor. Make sure that your back is straight but not rigid. Your palms are resting on your thighs. If you are sitting on a chair, your feet should be planted on the floor. Make sure you do not slouch. You might want to use some lower back support. The key here is to find a position that you are willing to commit to for the duration of your meditation without inviting you to sleep.

4. Close your eyes, take a few deep breaths, slow, long, and relaxed. Take a moment to notice the noises in the room and the smells in the room. Feel your body as it rests on the chair. Notice all sensations outside and inside your body. Do not look for them, do not dwell on them, just notice them as they come up and gently let them go. Some will not leave easily (like an itch or an ache) but continue to notice them and then let them go again. Gently, do not force anything.

5. Focus your attention on the sensation of your breath at your nostrils, how it comes in and how it goes out. Just watch it. Don't force it, don't follow your breath, just notice it as it comes in and out again and again. It is a very gentle process of noticing without any judgment. Just let it happen and observe, witness it.

6. Now as you inhale through your nose silently say the sound SOO, then slowly exhale through your nose while silently saying HUM. Continue to allow your breath to flow easily, silently repeating So. . . Hum . . . with each inflow and outflow of the breath. You don't need to keep the mantra pegged to the breath after the first few times.

7. There is no particular rhythm or pace to the mantra, just let it do what it wants to do. Repeat it at whatever speed or pace you are driven to do.

8. As your mind wanders away from your mantra—which will happen—notice where it has gone, and gently bring your attention back to your mantra. Just let the thought go and return to your mantra.

9. When physical sensations, noises in the room, or emotions take you away from the mantra—which will happen—and you notice it, gently bring your attention back to your mantra.

10. When your attention drifts away and you are lost in thought, daydreaming, miles away from your chair—which will happen—notice it, look at your daydream, and gently let it go. Go back to noticing your mantra again and again.

11. When the voice in your head starts telling you that you are doing it all wrong, that you are a loser, that you cannot even meditate—which will happen—notice the voice and gently go back to your mantra.

12. When your back starts to hurt and your knee starts to ache, don't be tempted to change positions. Today you committed to this seat, tomorrow you can pick another. Notice the discomfort and, unless it is excruciating, choose to go back to your mantra. If it continues to be uncomfortable, choose to change position with mindfulness of what you are doing and go back to your mantra.

13. Do this process of losing your attention again and again and gently bringing it back to your mantra again and again, without judgment. You are not failing. This is how you meditate, how you practice the muscle of your attention to stay focused where you want it to focus: on your mantra. Repeat the process again and again. Keep the process going until the alarm goes off.

14. When the alarm goes off, take a slow deep breath, keep your eyes closed, stop repeating the mantra, and just sit there for a moment in total silence without a thought.

15. When you are ready, open your eyes and smile at your Self. You are meditating—you are doing something great for yourself!

(If you prefer to listen to the guided mantra meditation you can find it in my website: www.monicabelizan.com under Guided Meditations.)

FURTHER READING

These are some of the writers I have referred to throughout this book and whose works you may also find illuminating.

Jack Kornfield, *A Lamp in the Darkness: Illuminating the Path Through Difficult Times* (Sounds True, Boulder, CO: 2014).

Matthieu Ricard "The Lama in the Lab," *Shambhala Sun*, March 2003.

Dan Harris, *10% Happier: How I Tamed the Voice in My Head, Reduced Stress Without Losing My Edge, and Found Self-Help That Actually Works--A True Story* (Harper Collins: 2014).

Deepak Chopra, *The Spontaneous Fulfillment of Desire: Harnessing the Infinite Power of Coincidence* (Harmony: 2004).

Deepak Chopra & Rudolph Tanzi, *Super Genes—Unlock the Astonishing Power of Your DNA for Optimum Health and Well-Being* (Harmony Books: 2015).

Eckhart Tolle, *The Power of Now: A Guide to Spiritual Enlightenment* (New World Library, Novato California: 1997).

Gregg Braden, *The Divine Matrix: Bridging Time, Space, Miracles, and Belief* (Hay House: 2008).

Gregg Braden, *The Spontaneous Healing of Belief—Shattering the Paradigm of False Limits* (Hay House: 2008).

Neville Goddard, *The Power of Awareness* (Penguin: 1952).

Neville Goddard, *Awakened Imagination* (Penguin: 1954).

DAVIDJI, *Secrets of Meditation. A Practical Guide to Inner Peace and Personal Transformation* (Hay House: 2012).

Marianne Williamson, *The Law of Divine Compensation: On Work, Money, and Miracles* (HarperOne: 2014).

Marianne Williamson, *A Return to Love: Reflections on the Principles of "A Course in Miracles"* (HarperOne: 1996).

Dr. Wayne W. Dyer, *The Shift. Taking your Life from Ambition to Meaning* (Hay House: 2010).

Mallika Chopra, *Living with Intent. My Somehow Messy Journey to Purpose, Peace and Joy* (Harmony: 2015).

A Course in Miracles (Huntington Station, NY: Foundation for Inner Peace, 1975).

Deepak Chopra: I encourage you to read as many of Deepak's books as you can. Each one of them delivers a jewel of information and compassionate teaching in a style that is uniquely poetic and elegant. Here are a few of my favorite ones:

The Seven Spiritual Laws of Success

The Book of Secrets

Reinventing the Body, Resurrecting the Soul

The Ultimate Happiness Prescription

Printed in the United States
By Bookmasters